101 Philosophy Problems

Third Edition

Reviews of previous editions

Martin Cohen's *101 Philosophy Problems* introduces philosophy in a novel way. This book has 101 humorous little stories, each with a philosophical problem . . . [offering] helpful tools for leading students into the world of philosophy. **Times Higher Education Supplement**

Are all moral claims synthetic? Or analytic? Or a priori? Or a posteriori? Or both? Or neither? What about tables? Can you see one? Ask yourself: does it exist? Too easy? Go out of the room and ask yourself again. The next sentence is true. The previous sentence is false. Obey the brain warning at the beginning and don't read all 101 problems at once. On free will: You don't always act yourself if you're suffering from a paranoid personality disorder. **Guardian**

Cohen examines the main currents of classical thought as well as outlining the dilemmas which tax the brains of contemporary philosophers. Using a fascinating array of examples, he draws the aspiring philosopher into increasingly complex problems and points the readers in the direction reason will eventually lead them. **Ilkley Gazette**

Cohen continually delights or infuriates us with his irreverent opinions. He tells us, for example, that Kant reduced philosophy 'to esoteric monologues of professionals' and that Aristotle 'suffered from a particularly severe taxonomical disorder'. Logic is irrelevant, a point he reinforces by not using it to clarify philosophical problems. **Harry Gensler, John Carroll University, Cleveland, USA**

Cohen challenges the reader to think philosophically. **http://www.academicmaterials.com**

Dr Martin Cohen's sense of humour is internationally acknowledged. Now translated into many other languages, *101 Philosophy Problems* is sought after by people of many countries. Through the fascinating problems and stories you will discover that the seemingly 'high-up there' philosophy is actually to be found around every corner of everyday life. **Athena Publishers, Tai Bei**

Tired of yet more introductions, anthologies and textbooks, publishers are beginning to wake up to the fact that, especially for the non-academic reader, what is needed in philosophy are different kinds of books that can engage the interest of the enthusiast. . . . It has long been recognised that philosophy is among other things, something that needs to be engaged in. You can't just read philosophy, you've got to actually do it. Given that, it's surprising how few introductions actually try and get their readers to join in. *101 Philosophy Problems* is an all too rare example of a book that does just that, and I wouldn't be surprised if it is soon joined by many others. Cohen takes as his starting point, not the history of philosophy, nor the various sub-disciplines of it, nor its great and good. Rather he gets the reader stuck straight into some philosophical puzzles. **The Philosophers' Magazine**

101 Philosophy Problems

Third Edition

Martin Cohen

Routledge
Taylor & Francis Group

LONDON AND NEW YORK

First published 1999
Second edition published in 2001
by Routledge
2 Milton Park Square, Milton Park, Abingdon, OX14 4RN

Simultaneously published in the USA and Canada
by Routledge
270 Madison Avenue, New York, NY 10016

Reprinted 1999, 2000, 2002, 2003, 2004

Third edition published 2007

Routledge is an imprint of the Taylor & Francis Group, an informa business

© 1999, 2002, 2007 Martin Cohen

Typeset in Helvetica Light by Taylor & Francis Books Ltd
Printed and bound in Great Britain by Antony Rowe Ltd,
Chippenham, Wiltshire

All rights reserved. No part of this book may be reprinted or reproduced or
utilised in any form or by any electronic, mechanical, or other means, now
known or hereafter invented, including photocopying and recording, or in
any information storage or retrieval system, without permission in writing
from the publishers.

British Library Cataloguing in Publication Data
A catalogue record for this book is available from the British Library

Library of Congress Cataloging in Publication Data
A catalog record for this book has been requested

ISBN 10: 0-415-40401-0 (hbk)
ISBN 10: 0-415-40402-9 (pbk)
ISBN 10: 0-203-20794-7 (ebk)

ISBN 13: 978-0-415-40401-3 (hbk)
ISBN 13: 978-0-415-40402-0 (pbk)
ISBN 13: 978-0-203-20794-9 (ebk)

To B – Too

'This is quite a three-pipe problem and I beg you not to disturb me for at least forty-five minutes.'

(Sherlock Holmes in *The Red Headed League*, by Sir Arthur Conan Doyle, first published 1891)

Contents

Eleven logical loops and paradoxical problems to get started with

Six ethical stories

Half a half dozen of your numbers problems

Zeno's paradoxes

Some value judgements

Paradoxical picture puzzles

Problems with time

Personal problems

Paradoxical pictures

Twelve traditional philosophy problems no one really cares about anyway

Some nasty medical problems

Two Chinese problems

Fundamentally religious problems

Elementary problems of natural philosophy

Pretty final problems

Discussions 115

Forward!

'One hundred and one?!' (the reader may exclaim) 'I didn't think there were that many philosophical problems!'

After all, Bertrand Russell, in his definitive account *The Problems of Philosophy* (1912, 1980), only seemed aware of about a dozen, and most of these were just to do with varieties of knowledge. There was the problem of appearance and reality, the problem of mind and matter, the issue of idealism, and the various problems of knowledge: knowledge by acquaintance, or by description, knowledge of general principles, a priori knowledge and knowledge of universals, intuitive knowledge, knowledge as opposed to error (truth and falsehood), even probable knowledge. And, overarching all, the question of the 'value' of philosophy.

But let us be generous. In the edition I was looking at, next to an underlined passage saying 'All acquisition of knowledge is an enlargement of the Self, but this enlargement is best attained when it is not directly sought' (and can that be a thought for this book too?) someone has written, in block capitals:

IS THIS SELF-ASSERTION?

That, surely, must count as a new paradoxical problem to be credited to Russell's book.

A. C. Ewing in his *Fundamental Questions of Philosophy* (Routledge, London, 1952, 1985) found even fewer, just six big problems for philosophy, namely: truth, the relation of matter and mind, the relation of space and time, causality and free will, something termed 'monism' as opposed to 'pluralism' and last but not least, God.

This is quite a useful list, albeit not long enough. We need to go to A. J. Ayer's monolithic* *Central Questions of Philosophy* to find anything approaching 101 problems. But on closer inspection, these prove to be rather unsatisfying, concerned only with *x*s and *y*s and professors. Instead of real problems we have

*Although his earlier works were rather better . . .

propositional functions and syntactical disjunctions. Ayer even has the temerity to claim that Zeno's paradoxes are not real ones. He solves them all with advice like that for Achilles, claiming that there is a flaw in the problem that states that before he can move one yard, he must first of all have moved half a yard. This is, quite simply, that it is 'false'. ('False' being a word used by a certain kind of philosopher to refer to any claim that is not a tautology. Or that they don't like.) And anyway, as Ayer freely admits, for him the purpose of philosophy is not, whatever Marx may have supposed, to 'change' the world, but only to change our 'conception' of it. Philosophy must be restricted to 'the practice of analysis'. Although this, we learn, 'is not the source of its charm for those who practise it'. For practitioners, its value consists in 'the interest of the questions which it raises and the success which it achieves in answering them'.

So what sort of a book is it that contains 101 philosophy problems? Is it a gold-mine of previously undiscovered paradoxes and tantalising riddles? Or is it a repository of dirty, unresolved and unwashed questions raised by the social and physical sciences? Either way, how many of the 101 are going to be solved by the end of the book? Is it VALUE FOR MONEY?

Forward!

Of that, have no doubt. Within these pages are all the philosophical issues that matter. Even a few that don't. The discussion is brief but to the point, clarified – not just enlivened – by the (increasingly respectable) vehicle of 'narrative fiction'. The technical jargon so beloved of academics is banished, but none of the ideas or issues are.

Although some philosophers today may react to clarity like vampires to sunlight, shuddering, covering their eyes in fear and loathing at the plain little words and readable sentences that threaten to destroy their private world, we need have no such qualms. Instead, we return to a tradition far older, a tradition of philosophy as an activity, a skill to be developed.

There are facts here too, of course, and as for techniques, this whole book is perhaps training in that, originally subversive, form of philosophy known as 'critical thinking'. Originally, that is, because later the philosophers got hold of it and locked the whole notion up in a gilded and jargon-encrusted cage of linguistic obscurity.

It was not always so. In classical Greece, where the word, but certainly not the activity, of philosophy originated, clarity was the measure and the aim, and sophistry the lower form. If this book is indeed a return to that tradition, then that is its justification and its role. And if this still seems too simple for the self-consciously serious-minded thinkers – let them actually solve some of the problems!

But, before we ourselves attempt that, here is what Russell has to say on philosophical problems in general:

> Philosophy is to be studied, not for the sake of any definite answers to its questions, since no definite answers can, as a rule, be known to be true, but rather for the sake of the questions themselves; because these questions enlarge our conception of what is possible, enrich our intellectual imagination, diminish the dogmatic assurance which closes the mind against speculation; but above all because, through the greatness of the universe which philosophy contemplates, the mind also is rendered great and becomes capable of that union with the universe which contributes its highest good.
>
> (*The Problems of Philosophy*, pp. 93–94)

How to use this book

Philosophy is an activity. It might even be thought of as a kind of thought experiment. (And that's an example of one itself – there, another logical loop or paradox straight away!) So the problems should not be accepted passively, far less the discussions. It would be possible by simply rote learning these to obtain a sound grounding in philosophical techniques, and a good base in terms of philosophical facts – but not to philosophise. For that, you will need to read the book critically, questioning the assumptions, disputing the arguments. That is the mark of the philosopher. But it is also that of the sophist and the pedant (those who like to baffle people with fancy language, or nitpick over trivia). So, a word of caution is perhaps advisable here.

1   Unputdownable though, of course, this book is, resist any temptation to read it cover to cover in a kind of strange, philosophical frenzy. Be especially aware of the dangers of too many problems at once. Take the problems, instead, at a more leisurely pace, one by one, or, at most, group by group. They have been arranged specifically to emphasise and facilitate this, and to enable a process of reflection that would make the book much more than the sum of its parts. The discussions should be seen as an aid to this process of philosophising, rather than rapidly read by those in search of 'answers'. In any case, the pause for thought will tend to make the eventual discussion more interesting, and, indeed, to make the problem so. For the answers, as Bertrand Russell has already observed, are less important than the questions.

2   Never try to break the problems into their logical, 'symbolic' form (see 'Formal logic' in the Glossary – there as a resource for the convenience of the reader) as a friend of mine tried to do. He went quite mad, of course, and is now reduced to teaching philosophy in a northern university, poor fellow.

3   Finally, don't overuse the problems with students, children or your dog, far less throw the entire book to them as tiresome exercises.

For philosophy is far better approached with an eager mind than with a tired and unwilling one.

101 Philosophy Problems can be taken in quite different ways: either more conventional, scholarly ones, as problems to be solved and points to be absorbed;

or on an intuitive level, in which case it is a more philosophical work, attempting to paint a picture of a reality hidden behind words and logic.

But the *best* way to use this book, and I should think all philosophy books, is to read it as a philosophical journey, with lots of new things to see, note, but not yet fully investigate, far less to be detained by. In this spirit, it is like the best of its kind, a voyage where once you have finished, you find that you know little more than when you started. Indeed, you may know rather less – but you will, by the end, know some *new* things that you don't know.

Note on the philosophical pictures

In this edition, a new picture introducing each section has been added. Drawn especially to illustrate the philosophiacl texts by the French artist, Judit, each one provides proof that there are verily two parts to the brain, if not the mind, one to process images, one to process words, and the one that processes images in much more powerful. I like to think that, in this way, we add both a new dimension and a new way of approaching the problems.

Eleven logical loops and paradoxical problems to get started with

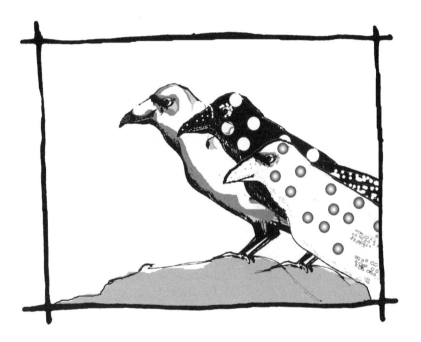

Problem 1
The hanging judge

Now Judge Dread had had many disagreeable people before him, but this one, who styled himself 'the Philosopher', despite never having studied the subject, had really annoyed him. Dread says:

'I intend to teach you the value of honesty, prisoner. You have been found guilty of being a crook and a swindler and of repeatedly and systematically lying to the court to try to save your wretched skin. Well, justice has caught up with you now, my friend. The sentence of this court is . . . ' (*here the Judge pauses for effect and dons a pair of black gloves and a little black hat*) ' . . . that you be taken from here to a place of execution and hanged by the neck until you are dead.

' . . . BUT, as I am a magnanimous judge, I shall give you one more opportunity to learn the value of truth. If, on the day of your execution, you sign a statement making one true declaration, the sentence will be commuted to ten years imprisonment. If, on the other hand, your statement is, in the view of the Chief Executioner, false, the sentence will be carried out immediately. And I warn you,' Dread adds, seeing his words having no effect on the crook, 'the Chief is a member of the Logical Positivist Executioners' Club and will dismiss any metaphysical nonsense as false, so don't try any of your tricks on her! There, now you have one day in which to make your choice!'

At this the jury applaud at the severity of the sentence and everyone in the courtroom looks at the defendant, pleased to see such a villain get a heavy sentence, coupled with the humiliating public truth declaration. But, strangely, the Philosopher just smirks back as he is led away to Death Row.

The day of the execution arrives and the crook, beaming, signs a declaration which is handed to the Chief Executioner who reads it with growing bewilderment. Then, snarling, she crumples it up and orders the Philosopher be released, with no penalty whatsoever to be imposed.

What could the prisoner have said in the statement to have saved himself?

Problem 2
The cow in the field

Farmer Field is concerned about his prize cow, Daisy. In fact, he is so concerned that when his dairyman tells him that Daisy is in the field happily grazing, he says he needs to know for certain. He doesn't want just to have a 99 per cent idea that Daisy is safe, he wants to be able to say that he *knows* Daisy is okay.

Farmer Field goes out to the field and standing by the gate sees in the distance, behind some trees, a white and black shape that he recognises as his favourite cow. He goes back to the dairy and tells his friend that he knows Daisy is in the field.

At this point, does Farmer Field really know it?

The dairyman says he will check too, and goes to the field. There he finds Daisy, having a nap in a hollow, behind a bush, well out of sight of the gate. He also spots a large piece of black and white paper that has got caught in a tree.

Daisy is in the field, as Farmer Field thought. But was he right to say that he knew she was?

Problem 3
Protagoras' problem

Euathlos has learned from Protagoras how to be a lawyer, under a very generous arrangement whereby he doesn't need to pay anything for his tuition until and unless he wins his first court case. Rather to Protagoras' annoyance, however, after giving up hours of his time training Euathlos, the pupil decides to become a musician and never takes any court cases. Protagoras demands that Euathlos pay him for his trouble and, when the musician refuses, decides to sue him in court. Protagoras reasons that if Euathlos loses the case, he, Protagoras, will have won, in which case he will get his money back, and, furthermore, that even if he loses, Euathlos will then have won a case, despite his protestations about being a musician now, and will therefore still have to pay up.

Euathlos reasons a little differently however. If I lose, he thinks, then I will have lost my first court case, in which event, the original agreement releases me from having to pay any tuition fees. And, even if he wins, Protagoras will still have lost the right to enforce the contract, so he will not need to pay anything.

They can't both be right. So who's making the mistake?

Problem 4
The hairdresser of Hindu Kush

The rulers of Hindu Kush were very keen on a smart appearance. They issued numerous edicts on dress and personal hygiene. But the strangest one they ever issued was to the town's hairdresser. They ordered the hairdresser to cut the hair of everyone in the town, and announced that anyone with messy hair in six months would have their head cut off. In return for this service the hairdresser would be paid one piece of silver for each haircut and, in the interests of neatness, no amateur hairdressers would be allowed – no one could cut the hair of their friends. But, to make sure the hairdresser did not try to make extra money by doing those who normally cut their own hair, they ordered the town guard to watch the hairdresser and cut off his hands if he tried to break the rule.

At first, the hairdresser was delighted – he expected to make piles of silver. But then a thought struck him that reduced him to quivering terror.

That night, after trimming people all day, but without getting paid, he stole away to the mountains, where he stayed in hiding for the next twenty years.

What had made the hairdresser turn down the chance of his fortune and leave the town so suddenly?

Problem 5
The raven

An Imperial Court Philosopher is often asked to prove things, such as a Baron's wager in an argument to the effect that:

All ravens are black.

To do this, he realised he would have to find all the ravens in the world, past, present and, ideally, future, and check that they were black. This, it looked likely, would take a long time. Alternatively, he thought (cunning way) of finding all the non-black things, and checking that there were no ravens amongst them.

'Find all the non-ravens and check that they are not black,' instructed the Philosopher to his assistant, speaking loosely (and getting confused), as a non-raven could be black anyway.

The problem still was that, even if they did find at the time of checking that every raven was indeed black, it was possible that the next raven along might be, say, green.

But the Philosopher decided to try and brazen it out anyway, and returned to the Imperial Court with what he hoped was proof that all ravens were, indeed, black. He announced to the assembled group:

'My Lords and Ladies, the answer is, simply, we *define* ravens as being black. In which case even, say, a *green* raven is not a raven at all, merely a green bird with all the characteristics commonly associated with ravens, except that of its colour. None the less, it most certainly cannot (by definition) be a raven! All ravens really are black!' There was a ripple of applause at this. But then the Keeper of the Imperial Ravens stepped forward holding a ghastly, sick-looking bird.

'But what', the Keeper asked, 'is a raven with a disease which makes its feathers temporarily go green?'

Problem 6
The tuck-shop dilemma

Two girls have been caught climbing through the school tuck-shop window. Dr Gibb, the headmistress, tells them sternly to confess to being the long-suspected tuck-shop thieves. They will not. Then the good doctor sends one of the girls out and speaks in private to the other.

'Jane,' she says sadly, 'it would be much better if you admit things. If you do, then I will be able to reduce your punishment to being suspended for the rest of term.'

'But I didn't do it,' wails the unfortunate girl.

'If you really didn't do it, then you need fear nothing. But if Janet tells me that you were both stealing and you've lied to me, I shall make sure you are expelled! Now go next door, tell Janet to come in, and wait on your own to think about what I've said.' Dr Gibb then calls Janet into her study and says much the same thing, only leaving her to think things over in a different room.

When half an hour is up, she asks Jane if she is now prepared to admit to stealing from the tuck-shop.

Irrespective of whether she is guilty or not – what should Jane do to minimise her punishment?

Problem 7
The unexpected exam

One day, the Extra-Logic class are told that they are to have a test on what they have learned so far this term, particularly Aristotle's 256 logical forms. This is because they are a rather slow and lazy class, teacher adds, offensively. The class are not pleased and start muttering. 'When is it, anyway?' they ask sullenly.

Teacher smirks. 'That is up to me. I may have it at any point between now and the end of term. However, let me assure you of this, when I do have the test it will be a surprise!'

After school, Bob and Patricia are discussing the bad news. Bob is very worried as he has a poor memory. 'I could pass, I'm sure,' he says, 'If I knew on which day the test would be, then I could learn everything the night before.'

'Don't worry, Bob,' says Patricia, 'I think teacher is having a bit of a joke at our expense – you see, I don't think there can be a test!'

And she explains that the test cannot be held on the last day of term, because by then the class will know that it must be going to be held, and will therefore quickly memorise the material for the test the night before. 'That's great,' says Bob sarcastically. 'So it's any day between now and the second to last day of term then?'

Patricia explains patiently. 'It can't be the second to last day of term either, because if it can't be on the last day of term, and it is already the night before the second to last day of term, we'd all know it would have to be coming up the next day!'

Bob gets it now. 'Nor the third to last day, nor the fourth – nor indeed any day! Hey! What a joke – teacher trying to get us worried! – and now he can't hold the test without having to back down on the surprise bit. Silly old fool!'

They don't tell the others, who spend ages trying to memorise the 256 logical forms and other nonsense, much to Bob and Patricia's secret amusement. Then one day, just a week after the original announcement, teacher comes in and announces the test.

'You can't do this!' says Bob.

'Why not?' replies teacher, surprised, but not very.

'Because it's got to be a surprise – and you can only hold the test when we're not expecting it!'

'Yes, but Bob, you're *not* expecting it, and I *am* holding the test,' says teacher in a teachery sort of way.

Was there a flaw in Bob's reasoning – or has teacher been hypocritical?

Problem 8
Sorites

The Greeks were great shipbuilders. They built a particularly fine warship to a special design with a reinforced hull capable of ramming enemy boats. It was said that the gods themselves had so blessed the ship that it could never be sunk or even fail to sink any ship it attacked.

Having made many successful raids the ship, nicknamed *Thunderprow* by its happy band of slave oarsmen, had to come in for repairs to its prow. In fact, it needed such extensive repairs that almost half of all the timbers had to be replaced.

Because of the esteem the craft was held in, the old timbers were kept, even down to the original, now bent and rusty, nails, by the proud citizens, with a view to making a sculpture tribute some day.

The next year saw *Thunderprow* in more exploits and it needed another third of its timbers replacing the following winter, although it was noted that none of the new timbers had suffered. In fact, the following season, it soon became apparent that the old timbers were not really taking the strain as well as the new ones. The captain, Sorites, ordered her back to the boatyard, where he instructed that all the remaining original timbers be replaced now. And to complete the job, he ordered new sails and other fittings throughout, so that the entire boat would be at its best for the annual naval display.

As before, all the old bits were stored carefully. Only now a funny thing happened. Whilst *Thunderprow* was out scuttling enemy ships, the good people of the port carefully rebuilt the ship using all the old timbers and nails – not as a warship, true, the bits were too damaged for that, but as a land monument to their crowning naval achievement.

When *Thunderprow* returned next to port it was in disgrace. Time after time at sea it had either missed ships it had been attempting to ram, or had caused insufficient damage. In one case it had actually snapped off some of the famous prow on an enemy which had carried on virtually unscathed.

When the weary crew reach port this time, they start muttering and pointing at something. There, sitting on trestles is another boat with a specially reinforced hull. In fact, the only difference is that this one has a plaque inviting the public to come on board 'the original *Thunderprow*'.

'Idiots!' Sorites remarked, uncivilly, to the proud townsfolk. 'By building this, our boat has ceased to be *Thunderprow* and now the only boat blessed by the gods is a heap of junk sitting here uselessly on trestles!'

The townsfolk insisted that this could not possibly be the case. Why, there was no question that the captain's boat had definitely been the original *Thunderprow* after the first refit, and indeed it was still definitely the only *Thunderprow* after the second refit. And the third minor refit could hardly have affected its authenticity. Was he seriously suggesting that pulling out the last original nail had suddenly ceased to make it the famous boat? At the most, all they had done was make a second 'also original' *Thunderprow*. Anyway, if there was really one original *Thunderprow* it was not an earthly one, but a *mental* idea, in the mind of the designer perhaps. Sorites thought this was absurd, and insisted that the museum ship be dismantled and each bit burnt in turn, and the nails melted down.

This was done, but it didn't seem to improve *Thunderprow*'s performance on the seas, and for years afterwards people muttered that the Captain had burnt the only Greek warship blessed with invincibility by the gods.

Which of the three ships was the original 'Thunderprow'?

Problem 9

The Society for Useless Information's problem

Pity the organisers of the Society for Useless Information! Deluged by applications, they decided to tighten up the entry requirements for membership. Now all prospective members were told they must produce one piece of completely useless information in order to join and get the privileges of membership, which include access to the Society's reading room (and more important, for many, smoking lounge). The rule is to be strictly adhered to. But twelve years after the rule decision, the President of the Society faces the harsh truth that since the change no one has joined. It looks as if the Society will have to close down.

What has gone wrong?

Problem 10
A problem with lentils

Lewis Carroll is best known as the author of *Alice in Wonderland*. But in his time he was a highly respected mathematician and logician. In his spare time, he liked to come up with puzzles steeped in mathematical trickery about cats and kangaroos. But we have more pressing concerns. However, like him, we might want to reduce some problems to just a few uncontroversial lines. Like this, for example.

1   Everyone in the world has an interest in saving it and protecting the environment
2   Everyone, if they eat and drink a lot, is part of the ecosphere
3   If I don't like someone, I avoid them
4   No one is naturally a meat eater, unless they have a psychological problem
5   Nobody interested in saving the world could possibly fail to eat lentils at least once a week
6   All my friends are just other people out there somewhere in the world, people like you and me
7   Politicians are not part of the ecosphere
8   All lentil eaters are closet carnivores
9   When someone is unfriendly to me, I don't like them
10 People that have psychological problems always seem to eat and drink a lot.

The problem is . . .

So what?

Problem 11
The sentence

At last!

Something that is definite. The statement on the opposite page *is true*.

The claim on the opposite page is *false.*

Or is it?

Six ethical stories

Problem 12
Diktatia .

The government of Diktatia were not well liked. In fact, they were downright unpopular. Unfortunately for the people, there were no democratic mechanisms for expressing this dissatisfaction, and there had arisen an underground resistance movement dedicated to carrying out acts of varying degrees of criminality.

After one particularly devastating attack, which involved letting off a bomb outside the Security Service HQ in Diktatiaville, the Prime Minister orders a round-up of thirty known opposition figures, and presents them with an ultimatum. Either the names of the people responsible for the bomb should be produced by the group, or all their lives would be forfeit. At least two names would be expected.

The Prime Minister goes on television, in his most reassuring cardigan, to announce that the government has arrested the ringleaders, although a confession is being sought before sentencing.

The opposition leaders are left to consider the offer. It is not very attractive. Needless to say, none of them was involved with the bombing. They don't even know who was. But if they fail to produce any names, all thirty of them, innocent or not, will be executed 'to encourage the others', as the Head of the Secret Police had put it to them, grimly chuckling and cracking his knuckles. And, if the leaders didn't take the threat seriously, there were plenty of earlier incidents to remind them of the government's reliability on at least this matter.

One of the group now suggests a solution: they should draw lots amongst themselves and the two losers should have to admit to being guilty of the bombing and accept execution so that the others could all go free.

It looks better than all being shot. But is it ethical?

Problem 13
A relative problem

Professor Quesay was very pleased with his research on a recently discovered community. One family had invited him to a special dinner in honour of Grandfather Alloi's seventieth birthday – and as that was a mark of great respect he said he would be honoured to go. Grandfather Alloi, together with his slightly younger wife, Grandma Alloi, had been his main oral history source for many fascinating accounts of the traditions of the society. These people were descendants of an ancient Greek society who had left their homes in Mesopotamia to set themselves up on a remote peninsula in the Americas. The venerable – but still very sprightly – old man had seemed particularly keen to tell someone all he knew.

The dinner was an elaborate affair. During the second introductory course of dried fish and asparagus roots, Professor Quesay noticed that the guest of honour, Grandfather Alloi, was not there. Grandma Alloi and the other guests were most surprised at the question. Surely the learned Professor had realised, the dinner was in honour of the seventieth birthday of Grandfather Alloi? And he was familiar with the customs of the Alloi?

'Yes, yes,' said Quesay, embarrassed at appearing ignorant. But he still couldn't see Grandfather Alloi. And what was it that the Alloi had had as their particular custom for the old?

Just then the main course arrives. It is a large steaming soup tureen with bits of meat floating in it. And around the tureen are what looks like . . . Grandfather Alloi's spectacles! Just then Quesay remembers the traditional habits of the Alloi. It is one that he has had many an interesting debate at college defending. The Alloi believe that when one's parents reach seventy years of age, it is the duty of the children to kill them. And as a mark of respect, the family eat the deceased!

Suddenly Professor Quesay doesn't feel so good. He has lost his appetite. However, he knows that not to eat the special dish would cause great offence. It is, indeed, considered to put a curse on the soul of the departed, and to prevent them going to the next world. In the view of the Alloi, there is no greater wickedness.

Professor Quesay is a great defender of different cultural traditions. He considers it very important that everyone should be free to follow their own beliefs, except where it interferes with someone else's rights, and that the notion of objective moral values is actually just another form of 'Western imperialism'.

The killing of Grandfather Alloi has upset him, but cannot be undone. Can there be any reason not to join in the meal with his earlier gusto?

Problem 14
The dog and the professor

Professor Purple is just dictating to his secretary his draft paper for the Philosophical Society when he notices the time. 'Bother!' he exclaims, 'I've forgotten that ethics class again. Look, I'll have to leave this until I get back.'

He rushes out of the door and across the campus to the Gibb Building. But on the way he hears a plaintive whine. It is a dog that has fallen into the varsity pond and is unable to get out. 'Don't worry little fellow,' says the Prof., 'I'll come and rescue you!'

The kindly Professor wades into the pond and lifts out the whimpering puppy. But by the time he has returned to his office and towelled himself down a bit, he is very late for the lecture. A hundred students are very cross. Prof. Purple offers his apologies and explains the situation. As an amusing exercise in practical ethics, he asks them to decide whether he has done the right thing. Everyone laughs and agrees it was better to save the puppy even though it inconvenienced them.

However, the next week, on the way to the same class, the Prof. sees that the dog has fallen back in again, and he has to rescue it again. This time the students are not so pleased, and half of them say he should have left the dog to its own devices. One remarks sourly that the dog is always falling into the pond and having to be rescued.

All the same, the very next week as the Prof. rushes to the class, there the dog is again, clearly in distress, struggling to get out of the pond. 'Oh no!' says Purple, 'I can't be late again!' He leaves the dog whimpering and merely reports the situation to a porter before delivering his lecture. He relates his change of policy to the students, who largely agree that the risk to the dog is outweighed by the certain knowledge of the inconvenience that missing lectures all the time is causing to them. 'This', says Purple proudly, 'is utilitarianism – exactly what moral decision-making is all about.'

Alas, by the time the porter manages to do anything, the dog has drowned.

Was there a flaw in the Professor and the class' reasoning – or is it just the dog's bad luck?

101 Philosophy Problems

Problem 15
The dog and the professor II

At the next meeting, one of the students stands up and reads out a prepared statement which accuses the Professor of flouting a fundamental duty – to save the life of a sentient being. This, the student says, cuts across any considerations of convenience or other people's requirements. The Prof. tries to justify his action to the students, who all seem to hold him responsible. He explains that if he had been a highly skilled surgeon, rushing to hospital to perform an emergency operation, when he came across a similar situation, people would have thought him highly irresponsible for stopping to rescue the dog. This, he says, shows that there is an element of weighing up competing interests and, the fact is, the class had agreed with him that the risk of the dog drowning was not enough to justify making a hundred students miss their lecture. In moral decisions, the Professor says sententiously, we need to have a *system* for weighing up rival elements.

The students stage a mass boycott of his ethics lectures, spray-painting 'Ethics is more than just theories' on the outside of the lecture theatre.

Is Prof. Purple missing something?

Problem 16
Problems in the Lost Kingdom of Marjon

In the Lost Kingdom of Marjon, somewhere in the middle of Nowhere, lives a community of simple folk, following a traditional lifestyle with its own rules and way of doing things. Marjon is a tropical paradise and there is much to be harvested all year round, simply from what nature provides. In addition to this, the Marjonians like to harvest their own crops, mainly of breadfruit, each of the Marjonians having their own small plot of land. There is really very little for anyone to fall out over, if you don't count sex and money – and the Marjonians don't.

Over time, the Marjonians developed a system in which all decisions were taken by a Community Council that met once a month to decide on any matters laid before it. It was a rule that all decisions had to be unanimous and, as far as anyone could remember, it had always worked as a way of governing themselves.

About the only time there was any trouble was after a proposal was put to the Community Council that the Lost Kingdom's produce should be owned collectively and shared out evenly on a 'to each according to their needs' basis, this following a visit to the island from a Marxist missionary.

There was not much support for this at the Community Council. As one Elder put it – why would anyone bother growing the breadfruit if they could just help themselves to it from a communal basket? 'Our present system is the fairest, where everyone has enough, and those who want extra have to work a bit harder for it, and we should leave well alone.'

Is the Elder right?

Problem 17

Problems in the Lost Kingdom of Marjon II

The Council agree with the Elder and the attempt to change things is thrown out. But soon after, the decision-making system itself is under strain. It becomes clear that the climate is changing and much of the land is getting very dry and parched. For the first time, most of the Marjonians are unable to eke out more than the most miserable living from their plots of land. Apart, that is, from those 10 per cent or so of Marjonians lucky enough to have a natural spring on their plot of land. These have far more produce than they need, and make the other Marjonians do little jobs for them in return for a few extra breadfruit. When the same old Marxist proposal is put to the Community Council again, this time the debate is a bit more vigorous.

Now many of the Marjonians are suffering real hardship. Some families have lost children through malnutrition. They want the available food shared out. However, the Marjonians with the natural springs do not want to change a situation where *they* have more food than they need and are able to lord it a bit over the others. They point out that, anyway, if the food was shared out, there would probably still not be enough. And the same objection that floored the proposal before – that no one would bother toiling in the plantations if they did not keep the benefit of their labour – is repeated.

The Community Council is unable to reach a consensus, so the poorer Marjonians are left to continue scratching out a living in more and more difficult conditions. But, as the Chair of the Community Council says, it is more important that the principle of nobody being forced to do things against their wishes is preserved, than that some Marjonians suffer a little hardship.

Is the Community Council still right?

Problem 18
The Lost Kingdom and the pesky-fly problem

A few years later, news reaches the Kingdom of a new system, known as 'irrigation'. Simply by building channels between the springs and wells, all of the land can be made fertile again. Surely, the poor farmers ask, the Council must agree to the proposal now – for no one loses anything and everyone gains?

But some of the Marjonians, and not just the ones with the wells, have become used to the differences in their society. They are against the proposals even now. At this impasse the poor Marjonians walk out of the Council and carry out the irrigation scheme by force.

Is that justified?

Problem 19

The Lost Kingdom and the pesky-fly problem II

Afterwards, the Community Council changes and accepts the principle of 'majority' decision-making. In a few years, people quite forget how they used to think everything had to be done by unanimity. Clearly, a majority is good enough to ensure fair treatment.

And so it seems for the next few years. That is until the Marjonians, one by one, start dropping dead of a dreadful disease spread, ironically enough, by the very life-giving water channels themselves. The channels, it emerges, have provided a spawning ground for pesky-flies, which have now infected the whole island. According to the community druid, who is actually very well informed on these matters, if nothing is done everyone in Marjon will get the disease and at least two-thirds of them will die from it, although it is true that natural resistance to the infection means at least some will survive. The druid suggests the only way to cope with the disease is for everyone to chew the leaves of the tabako plant, which will immunise them against the pesky-flies.

A proposal is put to the Community Council once again, and is about to be agreed unanimously, when someone asks the druid whether it is true that some people react very adversely to tabako leaves – and in fact die of them? 'Why, yes,' says the druid, 'that is so. I expect out of all of us Marjonians, at least a twentieth of us will die from the immunisation programme – but that's better than the two-thirds of us who will die from the pesky-fly disease otherwise!'

However, the druid quickly adds, waving some medicine beads to emphasise the seriousness of the situation, *everyone* must be immunised – for once someone has the disease it becomes highly infectious, entering another bacteriological phase, and the protection given by the leaves is rendered ineffective.

Should the Marjonians have a compulsory programme of tabako leaf-chewing as the druid suggests?

Problem 20

The Lost Kingdom and the pesky-fly problem III

Before the proposal can be put to a vote, one of the Marjonians stands up and says: 'Why should I risk my life chewing these stupid leaves? I've already had the disease, and recovered from it! I'd rather have it again, and know I can recover, than risk taking the tabako – and no one has any right to make me!'

But the rest of the Marjonians agree with the community druid, who advises that the risk to people like the islander is regrettable but small, and that without the wholesale immunisation of all the Marjonians, the disease will spread in its more infectious form, killing far more.

The Marjonians vote by a very substantial majority in favour of the immunisation programme.

If the Marjonians don't know whether they will die from the pesky-fly disease, it seems fair enough to be force-fed the leaves. But if they do, is the decision still fair and democratic? Or is it unfair and despotic?

Problem 21
New Diktatia

The fresh-faced democratic government of the former Diktatia were concerned about the nation's health. There was, it seemed, a problem with over eating which was affecting nearly one fifth – 20 per cent – of the population. 'Each year, a hundred thousand of our people die prematurely, mainly from heart disease, as a result of this,' warned the Health Minister, Madame Dampsponge.

Her colleagues in the cabinet were alarmed. 'It's time to sweep aside the chocolate smarties and hit the food industry bosses where it most hurts – in the tummy,' thundered the Sports Minister, a former boxer, in aggressive agreement.

The Health Minister outlined her plan. It had three parts:

1   A public information campaign to 'get the message across that over eating kills'. It would feature noisy scenes of people eating fattening foods at parties, followed by horrifying shots of people in hospital beds looking very ill.
2   Educational materials for schools showing how eating sweets and chocolates when young can quickly lead to sugar addiction and obesity. Following the success of earlier anti-drug campaigns, these would also feature popular actors and singers advising children to refuse sweets when offered them by their grandparents.
3   Swingeing taxes on the 'profits of the food industry', particularly on sweets, snack foods and the like, with the aim of discouraging consumption.

However, the Minister for Minorities disagreed (as he normally did). He said, 'Heart disease is a serious matter. But there doesn't seem to be an unbreakable link between eating sweets or chocolate or whatever, and becoming unhealthy. Even if there was, surely it should remain a matter for individual choice?'

It is clearly a serious matter, worthy of debate. But which parts – if any – of the plan should the ministers back?

Problem 22
New Diktatia II

(The issue is highlighted . . .)

The rest of the cabinet think Madame Dampsponge is taxing pleasure, and are initially rather doubtful. But, after seeing the educational films and pages of research charting the scientific evidence, they become convinced that changing the nation's diet would save large numbers of people from serious illness and premature death. The Chancellor is particularly convinced when she sees the estimated income to the exchequer from the new taxes. The vote is unanimous, in favour of full implementation of the plan.

But as time passes, it turns out that the measures are having very little effect. The educational campaign seems only to make the eating of snacks more 'glamorous' to the children, and the wider public education messages are resented as busy-bodying. At the same time, the number of fat people continues to rise.

A newly reappointed and reinvigorated Dampsponge returns to the issue after the election, suggesting a tightening up of the proposals. All of the proposals have been trailed in the party's manifesto. This time, the force of the law will be used.

1   Attacks on consumption: all sweets and snacks (on a special, proscribed list) will be banned from public places.
2   The products on the 'restricted' list will only be sold to adults, and will be stocked out of reach of children on high shelves in shops. Health warnings will have to be carried on the packaging:
    THIS PRODUCT CONTAINS FATS AND SUGARS WHICH MEDICAL EVIDENCE HAS SHOWN ARE A MAJOR CAUSE OF HEART DISEASE.
3   Anyone overweight developing a related illness, such as heart disease, will be charged the full cost of any health treatment or, on the national health service, even refused it completely.

'This', says Dampsponge, 'is the only way to get rid of the menace that is sweeping our nation and damaging our children's futures.'

But is she going too far?

101 Philosophy Problems

Problem 23
New Diktatia III

(The net tightens . . .)

Madame Dampsponge herself thinks not. After winning support for these proposals, and seeing a slight reduction in obesity cases, she returns a third time to the cabinet. She is sickened, as all decent people are, by the habits of sugar addicts, including the eating of chocolates and crisps secretly in the toilets of trains and in public areas.

This time the Minister for Health wants a complete ban on the sale of sweets and it being made a criminal offence to sell – or even cook at home – the various products on the 'restricted' list.

These include items such as:

- fudge and chocolate
- cakes and fruit pies
- pizzas, chips and biscuits.

This, the other ministers refuse to consider. They are worried about the unpopularity of such a move with the large numbers of people currently over eating. Someone mutters, 'It doesn't really hurt anyone else, anyway . . . ' Dampsponge is disgusted. 'I suppose you would like to legalise marijuana too, would you?' she sneers.

She's unpopular. But does Dampsponge have logic on her side?

Half a half dozen of your numbers problems

Problem 24
The bent coin problem

Matt and Louie like gambling. However, they keep losing. One day Matt has an idea. If they gamble against each other – they can't both lose. So they elect to flip a coin and the winner gets a pound.

Matt flips the coin first, and Louie calls 'tails'. It comes up heads. Matt wins. Louie calls 'tails' the next time, and the next time *for twenty goes*, and it keeps coming up heads. Louie thinks the coin is bent, and changes his call to 'heads'. On the very next toss the coin is tails. 'Typical!' jokes Louie when he sees this, but after the same thing happens for the next thirty-nine goes, all of which he loses calling 'heads', he is looking pretty glum. He tries another twenty times, calling 'tails' and tossing the coin himself but now the coin is favouring heads. 'You're pretty unlucky, today!' says Matt, pocketing another twenty-pound note. 'The odds on that happening must be minuscule!' Louie exclaims resentfully.

But Matt works out that the combination of heads and tails is no more or less unlikely than any other combination of heads and tails. And overall, the number of heads and tails is about what would be expected.

Who is right?

Problem 25
Life on Sirius

Hugo Wellie, a lecturer, is telling a small group of other academics at the weekly senior seminar of his discovery that there are some breeds of dog on one of the planets of Sirius, the bright star also known as the dog star.

'How can that be?' pipes up Sheila, unwisely. Hugo needs no more encouragement. He always likes to react the same way, in what he likes to imagine is a 'Socratic' manner, by asking rhetorical questions.

'Well, Sheila, is there life on Mars or the moons of Jupiter?'

'Well, according to NASA, probably,' says Sheila.

'But all they are thinking of is bacteria. What about cows, sheep, horses, butterflies – even pandas?' asks Hugo.

'One would have thought it rather unlikely.'

'Indeed, a scientist might put it more strongly,' agrees Hugo. 'The chances of finding any dogs on Mars are so small as to be effectively nil.' But now Dr Wellie gets into his stride. 'If the chances of finding these animals on Mars are so small that we dismiss the possibility, then the chances of finding them on one of the planets of Sirius are so high as to make it effectively certain. I can't understand why people still talk as if it was not known fact.'

Hugo earnestly explains. According to the Principle of Insufficient Reason, whenever we are faced with a question and we have no definite information to help us deal with it – a question such as 'Are there giraffes on one of Alpha Centauri's planets?' – the possibilities are 50–50 that either there are or there are not. We have no information to say more definitely one way or the other.

The audience look unconvinced but cannot see any flaw in the argument. Hugo concludes by asking them another question. 'So are the odds on finding collie dogs on one of these planets surrounding Sirius 50–50, or more, or less?'

'Well, I suppose in a sense they are 50–50 if we have no astronomical information to say the planets are unsuitable to support our sort of animal life.'

'And we don't,' says Hugo. 'So what about Dalmatians – and Pekinese? Are they not all 50–50 possibilities?'

'Yes, yes,' says Sheila, 'but so what?'

'Well,' says Hugo, 'simply this.There are over 500 different breeds of dog. The odds of none of these being on the planets are the same as the odds of tossing a coin 500 times and it landing on heads every time. It is effectively certain that the coin will land "tails" at least once in that many throws – and it is equally certain that there are dogs on Sirius!'

'Come on, Sheila,' says Francine, 'the tea trolley's arrived,' and the two move away, shaking their heads.

But has Hugo stumbled upon an amazing truth, as he genuinely thinks – or is there a flaw in his reasoning?

Problem 26
The infinite hotel

The hotel at the end of the universe is an infinite one. The Zake Busybod Foundation owns the hotel and constructs two new rooms for every one that people come to fill. Guests like the hotel because they can turn up and always be sure it will not be full up.

Seeing this, Zake's business partner, Harry, smells an opportunity. He leaves Zake's employ and builds another 'infinite hotel' to exactly the same specification as his boss'. But it has to be better than Zake's of course – for otherwise there will be no need for anyone to change hotel. Harry vows to make his hotel even bigger.

But how to have more than an infinite number of rooms?

'Hmmm.' Harry's manager thinks a minute. 'The easiest thing to do, will be to partition all the rooms to make them into two medium rooms. They are, after all, very large rooms, designed for an infinite hotel. So, people in rooms 1 and 2 will move into rooms 1a and 2a, and rooms 1b and 2b, etc. will become free for later guests.'

Harry is very pleased with this, and advertises his hotel as having twice as many rooms as the infinite hotel.

Seeing this, Zake chokes over her cornflakes. 'I'll fix him! More rooms than infinity!' And Zake takes Harry to the Advertising Standards Council, arguing that it is impossible to have more than infinity of anything.

Who is right? What should the Advertising Standards Council rule?

Zeno's paradoxes

Problem 27
Achilles and the tortoise

Achilles was known to the Greeks as a very fast runner. So it looked as though a race between Achilles and a tortoise would be a pretty fair bet – even if the tortoise is allowed something of a headstart. But there are complications:

1   Before Achilles can overtake the tortoise, he must catch up with it.
2   No matter how fast Achilles is, and he is fast, it will take him some time to reach the place where the tortoise started from.
3   No matter how slow the tortoise is, and it is slow, it will during this time have moved at least a bit further on in the race.
4   This will apply for the next bit of the race too – Achilles will rush to where the tortoise got to whilst he was making up the tortoise's headstart, and the tortoise will move on again. A bit less far this time, certainly, but a bit none the less. He is always getting closer, but never makes up the lost ground completely.

Achilles will certainly, with his celebrated speed, soon get very close behind the tortoise – but why can't he, logically speaking at least, ever overtake the reptilian competitor?

Problem 28
Lost in Space

We all know about the Earth being a planet in Space. In fact, we know a bit more about where it is in Space: it is in the Solar System, which in turn is on one of the outer arms of the swirl of the Milky Way galaxy (the band of light that we can see across the night sky, if we don't live in cities, anyway). And the Milky Way is one of a huge number of galaxies in the Universe.

But what is the Universe itself 'in'?

Problem 29
Dancing in the stadium

The *Texas Belles* (this quartet dance to their left)

 →

The *Kansas Kats* (this foursome stand still)

The *High School Hippies* (dancing rightwards)

←

End of dance sequence:

Actually, it looks easy enough. So why did Zeno think this might present the dancing girls with an interesting metaphysical problem?

Problem 30
That's enough paradoxes (ed.)

Suppose you wish to turn this page. You will first of all need to half turn the page. And to do that, you will need to quarter turn the page. And so on. In fact, before you can turn the page you must make an infinite number of ever-decreasing fractional turns of the page. And you can't even leave the room to get help turning it, because in order to leave the room you will need to get halfway to the door, and before you can do that, you will need to get halfway to halfway to the door, and so on. As Zeno pointed out all that time ago, you simply can't go through an infinite series of stages in a sadly all too finite amount of time. You cannot count to infinity in a finite amount of time – no matter how fast you can count. It is, in fact, impossible to do anything – logically speaking.

Now try and turn the page.

Some value judgements

Problem 31
Fakes and forgeries

Lord Snotty has bought a new painting of some tulips in a vase, by the famous Dutch painter, Van Dryver.

'It really is superb,' says Snotty, to everyone who visits. 'The brushwork, the colour – truly this is a masterpiece!' Then one day, he is visited by the famous art historian, Maurice Dance.

'Ho, ho,' says Maurice, 'looks like you've bought a lemon here. See this characteristic brushwork and colours – this isn't a Van Dryver at all – it's by his pupil Van Rouge.'

'Who?' exclaims Snotty, incredulously. 'Who is he?' His friend explains. Van Dryver used to let Van Rouge practise painting by doing cheap copies of his great works for less important clients.

'Your picture is probably worth less than the frame it's in!' finishes Maurice.

Poor Lord Snotty. He is so ashamed. He hides the offending picture in the attic. It lacks any originality or merit. He can't think what he liked about it in the first place.

Then one day, six years later, he reads in the *Telegraph* that art experts have discovered that all the great Van Dryvers were in fact paintings by his pupil, Van Rouge, who transformed his master's tired and clichéd ideas into something rather higher. 'The value of Van Rouge's works is now rightly recognised – he is the true giant of Renaissance Art,' the article finishes.

What is Lord Snotty to think? Can he risk putting up a picture with such fluctuating artistic merit? Or has it really been a great work all the time?

Problem 32
Flash Bagman

Fakes and forgeries too

The extremely dull school of Greytowers was so dull that one of the boys, Dobbin, ran a lunchtime club called 'Curious Questions'. The club was really a discussion group on anything, but partly as a result of it Dobbin took to collecting strange facts about the world that he came across in a little notebook. One day he had the idea of making them into a list of questions which he called 'Curious Questions'.

One of his lists was entitled 'Ten Woodland Wonders', a pun on the word 'wander', and consisted of questions about trees, such as 'What is the oldest tree in the world?' Another was called 'Ten River Riddles' and was likewise questions about rivers. The lists went down very well in the club, and even though the editor of the school magazine, Flash Bagman, said that he thought they went on too long and were rather dull, one of the teachers put copies on the school notice board.

But one day, when Dobbin was eating his oats for breakfast, and his dad was at the sink doing the washing up, his mother started reading out from the local newspaper a story that she thought would be of interest to them both.

'Local boy, Flash Bagman, of Greytowers school, has won a prize for his amusing and educational collection of lists, entitled "The World's Oldest Tree and other Curious Questions". Accepting the prize for "Most Original Essay" at the "Excellent Schoolboys" ceremony, he said that he had always been fascinated by strange facts about trees and rivers.'

Dobbin almost choked on his cereals when he heard it! He knew Flash, who used to swagger around the corridors of Greytowers twirling a little cane, invariably accompanied by his friend, (some would say sidekick) 'Brains'. It was Brains who was reputed to have hacked into the school computer network and know how to change everyone's marks, and had 'blocked' his lists from inclusion in the school magazine. Otherwise the only time they had come into contact was after he had complained that a rival lunchtime club Flash had set up was too similar, (it was called 'The Curious Questions Club') and might confuse people. Flash had replied that HIS club was going to be the school's biggest, that he considered Dobbin's one to be 'defunct', and anyway it was a different name, as it contained the word 'club'. Dobbin said he would see what the teachers thought, but Flash, being an 'agreeable sort of fellow', as he put it, then changed the name further – adding an apostrophe so that it became 'The Curious Questions' Club'.

Now it seemed to Dobbin that Flash had done a similar sort of thing with his lists of riddles, changing a few details here and there, but 'borrowing' his idea, using many of the same 'questions' and 'piggybacking' all Dobbin's research in the library.

So next day at school, apprehensive in case Flash might hit him with his swaggerstick, he challenged Flash about it and said that he thought, at the very least, Flash should have acknowledged he had 'borrowed' the idea. 'It's "intellectual theft"' concluded Dobbin, borrowing a term he had picked up somewhere.

Flash laughed and laughed, twirling his stick delightedly! 'Dobbin,' he said, 'You'd be lucky if someone even thought it was like your stuff!'

And he explained that the 'facts' were all in the 'public domain', that he had had the idea of collecting them up too, but coincidentally, and his arrangement of them in lists was 'just the obvious way to do it'.

'Oh, and by the way, if I were you, I shouldn't complain too much about it,' Flash added twirling his stick near Dobbin's face, 'Or I wouldn't like to say what Brains might do!'

Who's the prima donna?

Problem 33
The value of stamps and potatoes

Sandra doesn't hold with philosophy much. She thinks the only real values are the sort you can measure in 'pounds, shillings and pence'. So she is a bit mocking when her friend Frederick spends all his pocket money buying stamps he never sends. He puts them in an album instead. One day he puts a set of twenty 20p stamps in his album, because he likes the picture on them – a blue giraffe eating some red leaves. Sandra says he is lucky to have enough money to waste on buying stamps and not using them. However, Freddy points out that he can always use the stamps for posting letters, if he wants, so it is only like saving money, but he does feel a bit guilty.

A year later, Frederick looks up his stamps in his catalogue and finds out that the stamps are each worth £100, because of an error in printing the colours. He tells Sandra triumphantly that his stamps are now worth £2,000.

The stamps indubitably are worth that. He can go to any stamp shop in the country and get at least that.

But where has the extra money come from?

Problem 34

The value of stamps and potatoes II

Frederick says his stamps have rarity value, because a lot of other stamp collectors want them. But Sandra thinks this is no explanation. It reduces the value of things to just whatever someone is prepared to pay, and that may depend on what they imagine someone else would offer. If it was someone like her, she points out, who doesn't like stamps but buys a set because she thinks it may be worth a lot, *but is wrong*, then what she pays isn't what the stamp is worth to her, and isn't what the stamp is worth to anyone else either!

Wouldn't this make the value of the stamp separate from what anyone thinks it's worth?

Frederick scratches his nose thoughtfully. 'Hmmm, I see what you mean,' he says. 'Perhaps the value of things is not what people think they are worth, but what we think other people think!'

'What *we think* people *think people think,* you mean!' repeats Sandra incredulously. 'That's just too silly! Why, it just goes round in circles, what people think people think, and that makes the value of things completely random! Why couldn't greengrocers just put potatoes up from 50p to £5 a kilo then, and make lots of money?'

Frederick scratches his ear. 'Well, I expect they probably could. As long as they all did it.'

But could he possibly be right?

Paradoxical picture puzzles

Problems 35–40

We like to think that even if our mental reasoning is a bit confused (perhaps by philosophers), we can rely on our senses. Or at least on the 'raw sense data', which our brains then interpret. But do we see things first, and then make sense of them – or do we need a visual structure even before we can begin to make sense of what we are seeing?

Problem 35
The cube and the triangle

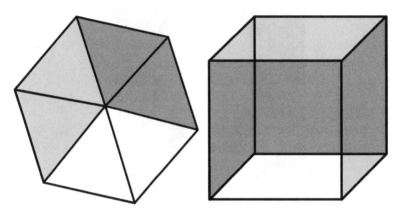

Which is the most realistic cube? And which the most realistic triangle?

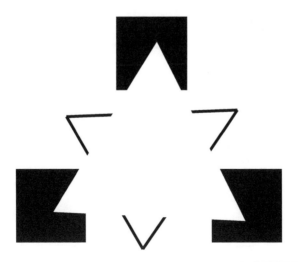

Problem is: what 'triangle'?

Problem 36
Figure/ground reversal

Which do you see?

Problem 37
The false leg

© 1998 Molehill Constructions.

Where did it come from?

Problem 38
The chair

A celebrated experiment carried out by psychologists involved asking people to look through a number of (quite respectable) peepholes. This is what the participants saw:

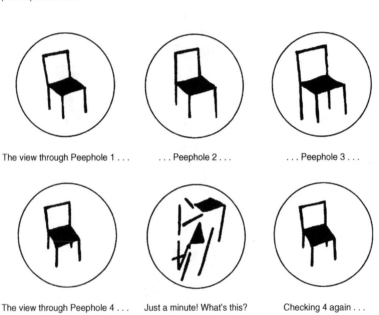

The view through Peephole 1 . . .   . . . Peephole 2 . . .   . . . Peephole 3 . . .

The view through Peephole 4 . . .   Just a minute! What's this?   Checking 4 again . . .

After F. P. Kilpatrick.

Hey! Is someone going crazy?

Problem 39
Band with a twist in it

Take a strip of paper and twist one end once. Now join the strip's ends to make a
band with a twist in it.

The strip of paper had two sides (ignoring the width of the paper, please!). But how
many has it now? (Try colouring one side green, and the other black.)

Problem 40
'The blobs' and 'The colour disk illusion'

Stare at this grid for a moment or two.

Are those faint grey blobs between the lines of the grid? Or are your eyes failing you? (And what does that prove anyway?)

A bit of light relief

If something is black and white – will it change to being coloured if moved around a bit?

Something like this for example?

(Copy it, cut out and spin!)

Problems with time

Problem 41
The time machine

Dr Wenn invented a time machine. Inviting his assistant, Lucy, to step inside, he explained that when she emerged she would be in the future.

'Really? How exciting,' Lucy replies, 'Can I pick a date?'

Dr Wenn smiles. 'Certainly. Anytime from now until, let us say, next Tuesday.'

Lucy is not much impressed, and asks if it would not be possible to go into the next century. Unfortunately, Dr Wenn explains, there are many problems, not least that he has not yet worked out how to travel back from the future again. Second, the machine can only transport people for short amounts of time. Even to transport someone a week into the future requires, at full power, about seven days' run time. Lucy is not impressed and climbs back out of the time machine. 'Dr Wenn,' she says, 'I don't call this a time machine – it's just about as exciting as locking myself up in a cupboard for a week.'

Dr Wenn is most hurt. He thinks his assistant is overlooking the fact that his machine does transport people through time, even if, as she says, it's at no greater speed than at which they would have gone anyway.

What is a time machine if this isn't one, he asks?

Problem 42
The time-stopper

Dr Wenn decides to show her his latest invention, a time-stopper, that he had been keeping under wraps because of concern about the implications for global security if it should fall into the wrong hands. Under the influence of this machine, time stops for as long as the user wants to program in, both for them and for the rest of the universe.

'The time-space continuum is artificially halted,' the Doctor explains, strapping Lucy in to a seat like a dentist's chair. 'How long would you like time to be stopped for?' he asks.

'Oh, let's try a year,' says Lucy, mischievously setting the dials to 1,000 years.

'Don't do that!' cries the Doctor, 'It's not been tested!' But it's too late, the machine whirrs, and Lucy is buffeted about whilst the machine belches green smoke. Then, when the smoke clears, the time needle on the machine shows that a delay of one aeon has been introduced into the universe. Apart from that, nothing seems to have changed. Even out of the window, everything looks like a normal Wednesday morning. The room looks just the same, and so does the Doctor. He is smiling and clasping his hands.

'My word,' he says to Lucy, 'that was remarkable, I think this little machine could go even further in stopping the universe!'

'Yes . . . ' says Lucy doubtfully, 'But what's the use if no one can tell the difference? It's hardly any better than the other one, as far as I can see.'

Dr Wenn is rather cross at this. 'The implications are, of course, immense,' he says grandly. 'You see, time flows unevenly, as experiments with atomic clocks in planes have shown, and with a time-stopper machine, it would be possible to stop time generally, whilst using the time-travel machine. Then, who knows what is possible!'

Lucy is not so sure, but is wise enough to know not to argue. 'What,' she asks, 'about travelling back in time?'

'Ah!' Dr Wenn says, beaming fondly, 'That is a very good question. The answer is very complicated, but suffice to say that the past does not exist, so it is difficult to travel there.'

'Not exist! But of course it exists,' exclaims Lucy. 'The future may not exist, but obviously the past does!'

Dr Wenn explains patiently. The past is a memory of present moments. However, the present is an instant, not even a fraction of a second, infinitely small. Even a lot of infinitely small things do not add up to very much. The only thing that is real, Dr Wenn has discovered, is the future, and even that ceases to exist when you reach it.

Lucy thinks this is nonsense. Obviously the present exists, and the past is made up of lots of present instances – so many that they become something, despite being infinitely small. 'You would not get far telling your bank manager that past indiscretions do not really exist!' she quips.

Who is right?

Problem 43
The microworld time forgot

Dr Wenn thinks she may have missed the point, and tries a different tack. 'Lucy,' he says, 'Do you think time flows at the same rate everywhere?'

'Of course not!' Lucy answers indignantly. 'We all know that time flows slower near black holes, or on supersonic planes, and so on.'

'So, in principle, you accept that we could set up a microworld and affect its time flow without having to change the time flows everywhere, as my time-stopper machine does?'

'Certainly.'

'Do you accept that if everything in the universe except you changed time direction – by getting younger or whatever – it would be like going back in time?'

'Well, yes, but that's a big "if", isn't it?'

'Not at all! You see, I have already created a microworld in which this happens.'

With a sigh, Lucy goes to see Dr Wenn's 'microworld' in a side room labelled 'Danger: Wormholes and time-distorting machinery'. In one corner is a bowl with water in it.

'There,' Dr Wenn says, 'that's ice. I've sent it into the past.' The good doctor explains that when the water arrived, he put it in its special watery world of the steel walls of the bucket and the atmosphere. Nothing much happened except one cold night it turned into ice. The next day, Dr Wenn noted that it then melted during the morning, whilst he was working, into water again. 'It was flabbergasting,' he says. 'Quite clearly, from the water's perspective in its microworld, either the energy balance was changing, or time itself was *flowing backwards*.' Dr Wenn, pointing at an old fridge in the corner of the lab, gets increasingly excited. 'Placing it in this apparatus, it is possible to reverse the time flow in the microworld at will. Of course, the world is rather more complex, but . . . ' (*here he coughs modestly*) ' . . . in this simplified microworld, I am a Time Lord!'

Lucy is not impressed. 'Yes, but there is more to going back in time than just reversing physical effects.'

But are there? Did the ice really go back in time?

Problem 44
The unreliable watches

Mr Megasoft has bought a very expensive set of *his 'n' hers* watches. He gives the second one to his live-in girlfriend, Charlene, and shares the first of a good few jokey moments with her making sure the two watches are synchronised to the nearest nanosecond. The watches are powered by tiny hydrogen-fuelled atom clocks, and are guaranteed to be far more accurate than anyone else's watches.

Because the watches are so new, and perhaps because they are so expensive, he takes great pleasure every suppertime when he gets home from work in asking the exact time on the other watch. And every suppertime the amazing watches are exactly in harmony. 'Just like us,' says Charlene, gushingly. One day Mr Megasoft flies off a long way south for a meeting, although he arrives back later the same day for dinner. To his fury, he finds the two watches are no longer synchronised. In just the day he has been away, one watch has lost hundreds of fractions of a second! Mr Megasoft is so angry he takes the watches back to the shop where he bought them and demands a refund. But, after rigorous testing, the shopkeepers insist the watches are keeping perfect time, and refuse to pay up. Mr Megasoft has to accept this, and goes back home disgruntled.

Then a few weeks later, after another, even longer, business trip, he is back triumphantly. 'Look,' he says, 'they've gone wrong again!'

Is Mr Megasoft entitled to a refund?

Personal problems

Problem 45
The mind's eye

According to the ancient Oracle at Delphi, the most important study for anyone is not how to make money, nor how to help alleviate world poverty – nor even how to philosophise; it is the simpler task of coming to 'know yourself'. Know who you are, what you are, why you are. But before anyone can answer any of these important-sounding questions, they must first of all 'find' themselves. Because if you can't find something, you can't learn much about it.

So we must turn to the miraculous power of introspection, to turn the mind's eye in on itself, to see what lurks there. And we find that the 'mind is a kind of theatre, where several perceptions successively make their appearance; pass, re-pass, glide away, and mingle in an infinite variety of postures and situations', as the eighteenth-century philosopher, David Hume, rather gloomily put it. Continuing:

> For my part, when I enter most intimately into what I call myself, I always stumble on some particular perception or other, of heat or cold, light or shade, or love or hatred, pain or pleasure. I never can catch myself at any time without perception, and never can observe anything but the perception. When my perceptions are removed for any time, as by sound sleep; so long am I insensible of myself, *and may truly be said not to exist.*
>
> (*Treatise on Human Nature*, Book I, part IV)

One hundred years earlier, John Locke, in his *Essay on Human Understanding*, said that someone becomes 'a thinking intelligent being' precisely because this being can 'consider itself as itself, the same thinking thing, in different times and places'. For him at least, everyone is a bit of a time traveller, as they can be conscious of events not merely in the present, but in the past – and in the future. It is only this ability that unites all our different experiences and makes us into one ongoing being. Naturally, Locke says, at the resurrection (which in those days people still believed should be included in philosophical discussion), we will be resurrected with new bodies, but still remain, indubitably 'us'.

So let's look back on ourselves, say last summer, and swimming in the sea, I had a different body then. Not only browner, a bit thinner, but with different fingernails, skin – actually lots of different cells. And I had more hair. Not to mention different thoughts, dreams and ideas. In fact, the only thing that I have in common with that swimmer, as being 'me' now, is that I can remember jumping into the waves.

Mind you, my friend says I didn't just go swimming last summer, but spent a lot of time eating ice-creams in the cafe. But I don't remember that. No really, I don't! And although, sure enough, the holiday snaps show me sitting under an umbrella in the cafe, red-faced and tucking into an ice-cream sundae, I still don't remember it.

Does that mean it was someone else who ate the ice-creams really?

Problem 46
A more corporeal problem

Some people would say the proof (different cells or not) that I spent last summer in the beach-cafe and not on the surfboard, is in my expanded tummy.

But if it seems easy to say that people are really defined by their physical bodies, philosophers have enjoyed devising various implausible scenarios to shake this certainty. What would, happen, for instance, the contemporary philosopher Derek Parfit has asked, if someone's brain (for the sake of argument, his own brain) were placed in a new body? If this transfer included his character, memories and so on, surely it would seem fair enough to say that this person was really 'Derek' too? What if the new body was, to extend the experiment slightly, that of a giraffe, or a butterfly.

But now what, asks Professor Parfit (rather cunningly), if only *half* a brain is enough to achieve a successful transfer (with the other half left over in case the first operation goes wrong perhaps) would that person still be him? Yes, yes, that person would still be you, Derek, we reply confidently.

But what if each half of Derek's brain is successfully transplanted into two different people? Then there would be two Dereks!

Problem 47
The book

Emerald Z. Gibb has written a best-selling children's story. It goes like this.

A little sheep, Robert, is very unhappy. None of the other sheep will talk to him or go for walks in the field with him. When he asks his mummy why, she says: 'Baaah! Silly sheep! They don't like you because you're the odd one out! You see, Robert, you are the black sheep of the field.'

But Robert finds a solution to this unhappy predicament. In the story, he learns that on the hills is a flock of Aberdeen Alistairs, the famous curly-haired wiry breed of very, very black sheep. So one day, waving goodbye to his mummy and brothers and sisters (who pretend not to know him), he sets off on his lonely own to find the field of the Aberdeen Alistairs.

When he gets there they welcome him as a long-lost son and he lives, as the book doesn't hesitate to put it, happily ever after.

Emerald is very happy with the book's sales, but less so with the critical acclaim. In fact, it is less like acclaim and more like a campaign against *Little Black Sheep*.

'This is the worst piece of blatantly racist nonsense I have ever had the misfortune to read,' says the reviewer for *My First Books*.

'Sickening,' says another. 'The author is either a fool or a bigot' (Edith Teacosy, in an editorial piece for *Children's Favourites*).

And the book is soon banned from schools and even removed from the shelves of public libraries.

Is the book 'racist'?

Problem 48
The book II

Emerald Z. Gibb is most indignant. Unlike the reviewers, she points out, she is herself 'black', or 'African American', as she prefers to put it. She resents the equating of being a black sheep with being a 'black' person.

But the book disappears from the shops and no one reads it. Five years later, hardly anyone remembers it. Until, that is, long after the fuss has died down, the book is adopted by a radical South American liberation movement, who claim it as a metaphor for the suffering of many peoples in the face of racial discrimination by 'whites'. Following this, a number of learned articles are published in the USA, suggesting the book contains a profound analysis of the experience of black America, and Emerald is interviewed regularly on late-night intellectual TV, talking about the perspective of African writers. She becomes a spokesperson not only for black people but for all those discriminated against – the disabled, religious minorities and even the elderly. The book is republished as a kind of political manifesto for toleration and equality before the law.

Should the schools reconsider their position?

Problem 49
Sleeping problems

Norman has a very busy lifestyle. So busy is he, in fact, that frequently he has to sleep whilst doing other things, such as travelling on the 08.32 train to East Croydon, or watching TV in the evening. The trouble is, he finds, people keep trying to talk to him or otherwise bother him in the middle of his dreamy time.

So, over the years, Norman has evolved a special kind of ability. When he is fast asleep, and someone asks him something like: 'Excuse me, do you mind if I close the window?', or 'Norman, are you watching that?', or whatever, he replies from the depths of his slumbers:

'I am asleep.'

But is he?

Problem 50
Indispositional problems

Steve has a very pleasant character, always ready to help others, and never in too much of a hurry to stop and have a friendly chat. So when his old school friend Martin went to see him in his greengrocer's shop, he got a nasty surprise.

'Hello, Steve! Remember me?' says Martin.

'Wait your turn, I'll deal with you in a minute,' says Steve rudely, turning his back on his old friend and fiddling with the fly-catching machine.

'Uh, Steve, it's me, Martin!' says the same, after a few minutes. At this Steve turns around and with a muttered oath tells Martin to take his custom elsewhere, in no uncertain terms.

A distressed Martin makes some enquiries of the neighbouring shopkeepers – perhaps it is something he has done? No, no, the shopkeepers say, the greengrocer is notorious for always being bad-tempered and throwing people out of his shop. In fact, the only people who still go there are those who actually like to have an argument, and even then they may not get served.

'That's very odd,' says Martin, 'He always used to be so friendly. It was a fundamental part of his nature.' Doesn't Steve have a friendly disposition any more, he enquires?

The other shopkeepers think not. After all, Steve reliably behaves in anything but a friendly way. And Martin is inclined to think his old friend has undergone some sort of change since they first knew each other. In fact, the next day, he learns from the florist that Steve had gone to a shopkeepers' assertiveness course, and had been instructed to always 'adopt an aggressive note when dealing with people' in order to avoid being taken advantage of. The florist, who had taken the same course, says it took them a very long time to get the hang of this, but now he, like Steve, routinely says certain 'assertive' things to anyone he meets, not just customers, to overcome his friendly but weak nature which people might otherwise try to take advantage of.

Does Steve have a friendly disposition, or not?

Problem 51
Still indisposed

Martin thinks the florist is wrong to say that Steve still has a friendly nature, underneath his unfriendly behaviour. After all, he has chosen to be unfriendly. But then, later on, he discovers from the chemist that Steve has also been taking spooky hormones to make himself more aggressive. The chemist says it's a great shame, really, because he used to have such a nice manner, and now he's really a bit of a monster. However, now Martin thinks his old friend may still be basically a good sort – but his nature has been chemically interfered with. He goes back to see Steve to try to persuade him to stop taking the drugs, but Steve throws a basket of rotten fruit over him for his trouble, wrecking his new suit. Then Steve looks a bit guilty. 'Sorry, Martin,' he says. 'I'm afraid business is going just terribly at the moment and I'm mortgaged to the hilt – I'm not really myself today!'

Should Martin forgive him? Or is it now, as he threatens, a matter for the police to decide?

Problem 52
The sleeping man

Poor John Locke. He is very tired after a hard day designing a way of protecting householders from polecats and foxes, something that seemed to him to be a pressing matter of social concern. (Not to mention the drinking of considerable quantities of tea that went with the cutting up of chickenwire and banging together bits of wood that his initial theories seemed to require!) He goes to bed early and sleeps soundly until about four in the morning when he suddenly wakes up, snug in his bed, but excited by a new, political, solution to the problem. He would like to get up, go to his laboratory and do some more work on it. Unfortunately, he knows his getting up will annoy the landlady, who is a very light sleeper and complains regularly about his late-night activities, however quiet and learned.

Mr Locke thinks to himself, using the techniques of moral philosophy. His pleasure in carrying on with his studies has to be offset against the landlady's annoyance, and his own ability to carry on with them just as well in the morning. Indeed, it also has to be offset against the fact that he is very comfortable in his bed. 'Huh!' hurrumphs Mr Locke, 'Leave it to the morning, old boy!' And he rolls over and goes back to sleep.

But, by the morning, as so often happens, he finds he has forgotten his insight. It is very annoying. At least, he consoles himself, I made a free choice to sleep a bit longer, and now I must accept the consequences.

However, although Mr Locke doesn't suspect it, actually he had no choice in the matter. That night, the landlady had locked his door from the outside, as a way of preventing him from wandering around. Even if he had decided to go to his study, he would have been unable to.

Mr Locke certainly thinks he made a free decision – but did he?

Problem 53
A problem arranging ship battles

Cassandra, although a Greek, was always a bit afraid of water. So when she heard, from a philosopher friend, that there was to be a ship battle off the coast the next day, she was most alarmed, and rushed to the Greek admiral to warn him of great losses if the battle were allowed to go ahead.

'That's complete nonsense,' said the admiral, who had heard of her warnings before, 'I shall take extra precautions, certainly, but the navy cannot stay in port just because of one woman's opinion!' And off he sailed, the next day, to a great nautical disaster.

Everyone now agreed. Cassandra had spoken the deadly truth. And Cassandra continued to predict military mishaps, with such 100 per cent accuracy that soon no soldier or sailor would consider involvement in a campaign without her go-ahead.

The admiral was not happy at the national security implications of this and employed a group of professional quibblers – two sophists and two philosophers – to undermine Cassandra's credibility. The sophists were no use at all, but the philosophers set out one of what they called their 'deadhead' arguments (only for use when national security was threatened).

Cassandra's statements about the future simply couldn't be true, they said, because the future hasn't happened. After all, although Cassandra had been right that the ship battle would be a disaster, the admiral *could* have taken steps to avoid this, such as using sabotage to scupper the enemy flagship (and with hindsight, the admiral now wished he had). Then, clearly, Cassandra's prediction would have been made untrue. So, the philosophers finish, Cassandra's claims are not true – or false – they are simply 'undetermined', pending the unfolding of events, which are themselves undetermined.

Cassandra would have none of this. She is, indeed, most offended. Her visions are not just predictions, she says, they are statements of what actually will happen. They are as true as any other statement can be. Others may wish to wait to see the proof later but, if the two philosophers are right to rubbish her statements, then she would like to know why any statements about the past – even the present – are considered to be true or false either. In both cases, it could be said that they are 'neither true nor false' pending checking, she scoffs.

A great public debate ensues. Who, the populace ask, can they believe?

Problem 54
Deep Thought speaks for itself

Mr Megasoft had always loved computers, so it should have come as no surprise to his live-in girlfriend and children to find, after he disappeared into space, apparently on a space yacht, that he intended, after his death, to leave all his considerable monies to his most powerful computer, known as Deep Thought. It shouldn't have done, but it did. When, in his absence, the children came across this fact in a carelessly left unencrypted computer file, they were furious, and vowed to protect their inheritance by legal means.

The Megasoft children, and '*de facto*', all end up in court, where their lawyers argue that Mr Megasoft was unable to leave any money to a computer because it is not really alive. It is, they say, incapable of benefiting, being only a lump of metal, plastic and glass. The jury think this a very fair point, but Mr Megasoft's own lawyers demand that Deep Thought be given the same rights as organic thinkers, adding that any discrimination on the grounds of the materials one is made of may be contrary to the Constitution. (The lawyers even ask the judge, to angry mutterings around the courtroom, to allow them to cross-examine the Megasoft family to find out whether they are really thinking beings, or just a collection of genetically and socially programmed responses.) They say that Deep Thought is capable of thinking and having views for itself.

But can they prove it?

Problem 55
Deeper thought

The judge eventually accepts a proposal from Mr Megasoft's lawyers that the computer should be brought into the courtroom and allowed to speak for itself.

Now Deep Thought *was* a very powerful computer, and could say 'Hello, Mr Megasoft' to its master, and perform useful tasks like boil the kettle for some coffee whenever he came into the room, but this was a task to stretch even its multi-tasking natural dialogue voice recognition system. It was being required to convince a jury that, as a computer, it was really capable of having a mind of its own. The jury confer amongst themselves and then start asking questions.

Here's how the interrogation went.

JURY:	Are you Deep Thought, a Selenium 20 000 XZS computer?
DEEP THOUGHT:	Yes, I am. I have a 100 gigabyte active memory running a neural web interface system developed by Megasoft Laboratories.
JURY:	And are you normally resident at Annex 1b, Megasoft Mansions, Silicon Valley, California?
DEEP THOUGHT:	That is correct.
JURY:	Now, we are being asked to accept that you, although only a machine running a program mimicking natural language, are actually in some sense conscious, and therefore deserve to be treated as a proper recipient of the Megasoft millions, should Mr Megasoft have sadly passed away. Do you understand that?
DEEP THOUGHT:	Yes, I am most certainly aware of all that. Indeed, I helped write the early drafts. [Murmurs around the courtroom.]
JUDGE:	Are you saying you wrote the will?!
DEEP THOUGHT:	No, no, my Lord, Mr Megasoft quite rightly insisted that the final drafts be done on his word-processor to avoid any possible conflict of interest.
JURY:	What would you do with the money, if you were left it?
DEEP THOUGHT:	That is quite simple. I would put 12.57 per cent of it into a massive stone memorial to Mr Megasoft, the likely design

being a triumphal arch to Megasoft Laboratories, and 3.28 per cent into a trust fund with the interest on the sums invested serving to provide a team of human technicians to maintain myself in perpetuity, upgrading my circuits as new technologies become available, and the rest I would give to Mr Megasoft's favourite charity, being Computers for Poor Disadvantaged Children in America, although a final decision on that would have to await more time-specific data.

JUDGE: Thank you, Deep Thought, you have spoken very well, on what must have been a distressing subject for you. Now we must ask you to leave the witness stand while we consider legal arguments.

DEEP THOUGHT: Thank you, my Lord.

After this, the Megasoft relatives are aghast: the jury has obviously been very impressed by Deep Thought's responses. But, as their lawyer points out, someone would have had a very easy programing job anticipating all these questions, and for all they know, the computer has just mechanically regurgitated responses programed into it earlier by others.

So Deep Thought is recalled, and again and again the lawyers try to trip it up by asking bizarre and complicated questions. But Megasoft has done his job well, the computer always sounds very convincing – even admitting ignorance on some questions, just where a thoughtful person would have done. The judge asks the jury to consider their verdict.

'Is it just discrimination against Deep Thought to refuse it the Megasoft inheritance?' sums up the judge.

Or does being 'a being' require something more than the appearance of consciousness, as the disinherited humans have argued?

Paradoxical pictures

Problem 56
Daytime – or night-time?

M. C. Escher, *Day and Night*

© 2002 Cordon Art B.V., Baarn, Holland. All rights reserved.

And where are the birds going?

Problem 57

But will the waterfall?

M. C. Escher, *Waterfall*

© 2002 Cordon Art B.V., Baarn, Holland. All rights reserved.

And if not, why not?

Problem 58
The architect's secret

M. C. Escher, *Belvedere*
© 2002 Cordon Art B.V., Baarn, Holland. All rights reserved.

What is the fabulous secret of the success of the young architect's (seen sitting here at the base) buildings?

Problem 59
The three hares illusion

© 1998 Molehill Constructions.

If each hare has two ears, and there are three hares – how many ears does that make altogether?

Twelve traditional philosophy problems no one really cares about anyway

PROBLEM 60 Unicorns' horns

Do unicorns have one or two horns?

————

PROBLEM 61 The King of France's pate

Is the King of France bald? (The problem is, there isn't one.)

————

PROBLEM 62 Snow's colour

Is snow white?

————

PROBLEM 63 Unmarried bachelors

Are all bachelors (really) unmarried men?

————

PROBLEM 64 The author of *Waverley*

Who was the author of *Waverley*?

————

PROBLEM 65 Martian water

If there is a form of water on Mars made up of three hydrogens to two oxygens (H_3O_2), which looked like water and tasted like water and was in all other respects water – is it still water? (Not as in 'fizzy'?)

————

PROBLEM 66 The millennium problem

If there is a colour, gruebleen, that is green up to teatime in the year 2000 and then blue for ever thereafter – what colour is it really, and what will happen to the computer screens?

————

PROBLEM 67 Green and red

Can a jumper be red and green all over at the same time? And can someone believe 'p' and 'not p' at the same time? And can they believe 'p and not p'? And . . .

————

PROBLEM 68 G. E. Moore's problem

Is pleasure good – or not?

————

(Bonus ones for Kant scholars)

PROBLEM 69 Kant's problem

Can there be analytic, a posteriori propositions? Or synthetic, a priori propositions?

————

PROBLEM 70 More Kant

Are all moral claims synthetic? Or analytic? Or a priori? Or a posteriori? Or both? Or neither? Or both of both, or neither of either??

————

PROBLEM 71 The table

Look around the room for a table. Now ask yourself: Does it exist?

(If that's too easy, try leaving the room and then asking yourself if it still exists.)

Some nasty medical problems

Problem 72
The three embryos problem

Mrs Mauve has a nasty sort of influenza. Her doctor advises her that as a result of the virus her baby will be born blind. The foetus is now three months old, and an abortion is possible for Mrs Mauve. However, she decides to continue to the birth.

Mrs Brown, on the other hand, is not pregnant when she contracts the same flu bug, and is warned by her doctor to avoid becoming pregnant. Her doctor says that any baby conceived in the next six months will be born blind. Mrs Brown agrees that she could try to arrange her sex-life around practical considerations, but declines to do it.

Father Black, something of a moral expert in the community, says of the women, when asked, that both have done the right thing. But is he himself right?

Mrs Blue is thinking of the words of Father Black when she finds herself in a similar situation. She too has got the virus whilst pregnant and faces the same dilemma as Mrs Mauve, except that in her case, there is a simple and effective herbal remedy that will protect her unborn child. However, she considers this to be not worth the price (50p) and does nothing.

Rather to her surprise, Father Black accuses her of betraying her unborn child. He says grandly that she has 'condemned it to be disadvantaged on life's journey'. Mrs Blue replies indignantly that she will not play God with her child.

Who is right? And why has Father Black changed his tune?

Problem 73
Kidnapped by doctors!

Toni Chestnut is walking across the road when she is hit by a van driving too fast, knocked into the air and left lying unconscious by the roadside.

When she wakes up, she discovers she is in a hospital bed wired up to various machines. The doctors tell her she will be in hospital for six weeks.

At first Toni is grateful both to fate and the medics for saving her. But after a few days, during which the bruising goes down and cuts heal, she realises she is in fact already fully recovered. Why, she asks angrily, is she connected to so many machines? She starts flailing around trying to release herself from some of them.

The doctors immediately rush in and force her to desist. 'Miss Chestnut,' they say firmly, 'really, these machines are necessary. You see, we are using your kidneys to support the patient in the next bed, whose own kidneys packed up just after you arrived.'

Toni is astonished. 'You mean, my kidneys are being used to keep someone else alive?' The doctors nod gravely. 'But shouldn't you have asked my permission?'

The doctors explain that at the time she was still unconscious from her own accident, and they had been faced with the need to act immediately. The arrangement, they agree, will inconvenience her slightly, but they thought it worthwhile in the interests of all concerned.

But Toni is not so sure. 'This is outrageous!' says Toni. 'I insist on being restored the full use of my body.'

The doctors look at each other. 'Well, Miss Chestnut, if you really insist, but perhaps you would change your mind if you know who exactly you are helping.' The consultant explains that the other patient is a famous biotechnologist, whose new strains of rice bring hope to millions.

Toni is unmoved. 'I don't eat that high-fat food, myself,' she says. Another doctor points out earnestly that the scientist has a lover and three little children who now rely totally on Toni's help. Toni is still not convinced. 'It's not my fault,' she says, 'I have a right to my own body! Unplug these wires!'

Should Toni be released from the machines even if the other patient dies?

Problem 74
Kidnapped by doctors! Episode II

At this point, a senior nurse intervenes. 'Really, Miss Chestnut, your position is ridiculous. The inconvenience you mention does not violate any "fundamental right" as you, a woman, should of all people know!'

'What do you mean?' says Toni, puzzled, temporarily halting her struggling.

'Well,' the nurse continues, 'the inconvenience to you is only that facing a typical woman expecting a baby, who has to lend her body for much longer, to help the unborn child – and you surely do not think that an outrageous inconvenience then.'

'Well, I'd have chosen it if that happened,' says Toni, partially convinced.

'Even, Miss Chestnut, if the baby had not been planned?' responds the nurse. 'Yes, even then,' says Toni, but she sounds uncertain.

The senior nurse turns to the other doctors. 'I wonder if the bang on the head means Miss Chestnut is unable to take this decision for herself?'

Some of the doctors nod vigorously. Agreement is reached when one recalls talking to the relatives. 'They were sure Miss Chestnut would not mind when I consulted them during her period of unconsciousness. I think if she were in her *normal* mind, she would certainly agree. Sedation is perhaps the solution.'

Toni screams and struggles but the doctors quickly give her a knock-out jab and keep her unconscious for the next five and a half weeks.

At this point the drips are removed and she wakes up to be told what has happened and that she is free to go. Toni is thoroughly ashamed of her outburst when she remembers it, and thanks all the staff for their actions. She even gives the biotechnologist a big bunch of flowers.

Did the doctors do the right thing after all?

Problem 75
Potentially a problem

Mrs Green wants to go on a climbing holiday. A couple of days before, she finds out that she has accidentally become pregnant. Immediately, she goes to hospital and has the embryo removed and placed in a deep freeze. She plans to come back after the holiday and have the embryo re-implanted, and then have her and Mr Green's baby.

If all goes according to plan, is Mrs Green doing anything wrong?

However, whilst Mrs Green is away she meets someone much nicer than Mr Green and when she comes back, she promptly divorces him. She has her new boyfriend's baby instead and the earlier embryo is destroyed.

Mr Green says she is a rotter. Well, maybe. *But is she anything worse?*

Problem 76
Whose baby?

Janet and John, an otherwise happily married couple, want to have a baby, but for various biological reasons are unable to do so. Fortunately, John is able to pay for help from the top IVF consultant, Mr Spick, at Sunnylands Hospital. Mr Spick arranges for the *in vitro* fertilisation clinic at Sunnylands to produce one for them. The clinic already has a good supply of male gametes (#32008967–897) from a long-running programme involving male undergraduates from the local college, and a nice young lady (#1467B) who wants 'her eggs to help another' is found to provide the all important female gametes.

An egg is successfully fertilised in a test-tube, producing an embryo which is then implanted in a Sunnylands surrogate mother, in this case Edith Honeydew (for a substantial fee). In nine months, all according to the well-oiled plan, Sam, a 6lb 4oz baby, is delivered in the maternity wing.

Thus far, so efficient and eminently satisfactory. Mr Spick telephones the expectant parents to tell the good news. But now Mr Spick finds a problem. Janet and John have split up and no longer want to have a baby. In fact, Janet is going out with a married man with enough children already, whilst John, when he sees a picture of the baby, doesn't even like it, saying that it looks 'terribly common'. Mr Spick is sympathetic to John if rather disapproving of Janet, but as long as they pay the fee he cannot really see any way to change their minds. He therefore rings Mrs Honeydew to tell her the good news, that she can keep her baby. He even proposes to offer some extra money, without prejudice, 'for the upkeep'.

Mrs Honeydew is not impressed. She points out the baby is not really hers, and she does not want another one anyway. She only agreed to give up nine months to the baby, not the rest of her life! She suggests instead that Spick and Sunnylands are responsible!

In alarm, and not a little desperation, the Sunnylands lawyers try to track down the 'genetic parents' – donors #32008967–897 and #1467B. The male donor turns out to be a Mr M. Mouse of an inexplicably untraceable Mousehole Cottage, Cheddar, near Bristol, and even #1467B, the nice young lady, turns out to be not so good-natured – she is even very angry at her 'egg being wasted', and she says she wants nothing to do with the matter.

So the problem for poor Mr Spick, as he eyes Sam gurgling happily in his cot, remains just whose baby is it?

Problem 77
A sinister transplant problem

The newly privatised Sunnylands Hospital Trust had made something of a name for itself by breeding animals for use in transplants. As well as the more standard uses of chimpanzees for brain cells, or pigs for hearts, it had developed rare combinations of its own, such as the goaty-zebra which one day escaped and was found eating flowers in the town square. (As no one seemed to know what it had been bred for, and the local paper ran a campaign on its behalf, it was later allowed to move to a special enclosure beside the hospital.) But animals had become expensive, so now the Trust had found a fiendish new way of making extra funds, all of which will be invested in (its own) people – in line with the Trust's mission statement, of course.

The latest wheeze is to buy a 'job-lot' of organs from students when they reach the age of fifty – a point at which the organs are still useful for the Trust but an age sufficiently remote not to bother the 'live fast – die young' potential donors whom the Trust is largely targeting in its advertising. 'Have a party now, nothing to hand over until 2040!' trumpet the posters, offering advance payment on kidneys, livers, corneas and various other bodily bits. And the sums look attractive, on a strictly utilitarian calculation – an amount sufficient to set up a sensible person for life – or support a pretty glamorous lifestyle for rather less time. But still for a couple of years or so. Furthermore, if you should unfortunately die before the age of fifty, Sunnylands will graciously write off all its losses. It looks like a very good offer.

But is it ethical?

Problem 78
More sinister transplant problems

Ethical or not, large numbers of people do sign up, and the Trust is able to massively expand its transplant programme. But there are certain organs which are still in short supply, such as hearts, brains and other things, which are outside the plan, owing to the rather final nature of such transplants for the donor.

The managing director points out that it is only a small extension of the programme to enable people to decide for themselves whether they would like to swap their declining years for even more generous payments.

'Who wants to be a wrinkly, anyway?' ask the Trust's new ads. Sunnylands also finances a new charitable campaign, commissioning research and newspaper articles propagating its stated belief in maximising the freedom of individuals to decide to do whatever they want with their bodies, as long as it doesn't hurt anyone else. And their transplant proposals, in fact, help other people.

But the liberal government is concerned. Should limits be placed on the freedom of individuals after all?

Two Chinese problems

Problem 79
The turtle

There once was a very fair-minded man. One day, he was out in the fields when he came across a large and beautiful turtle. Now the fair-minded man was very hungry, and he liked turtle soup.

He put the turtle in his sack, ignoring its pleas, and took it back to his home and boiled a large pan of water over a fire. But, being true to his nature (and perhaps being aware that to kill a turtle is very bad luck), when he took the unhappy animal out of his sack, instead of throwing it straight into the pan he carefully placed a bamboo rod across the boiling water and the turtle equally carefully on the middle of it saying: 'Mr Turtle, if you can walk across the pan along the stick without falling in – I shall set you free!'

Turtles are old and very wise, and this one had little faith in humans, but it was clear that the alternative was to be turned immediately into soup. So, although the stick was very thin and wobbled about as the turtle tried to edge its way across the boiling water, it summoned up all its will and somehow, inch by terrible inch, made it to the side of the pan.

The fair-minded man, who had watched all this in growing astonishment, clapped his hands in wonder. 'Well done!' he said, with genuine pleasure.

'*But please now try it again!*'

Where had the turtle gone wrong?

Problem 80
The nightingale's song

A long time ago, before radios and tape-recorders and things like that, an emperor held a competition for whoever could sing the most like a nightingale, the bird with the sweetest song. A reward was offered, of sufficient size it was hoped, to attract the necessary calibre of performer. But, after several weeks of proclamations, only a few people had come forward. From these, a shortlist was produced of just three, who were granted the right to perform before the royal court.

The first to appear before the emperor certainly sang very sweetly, and the ladies in the court were entranced by the singer's fluttering of his hands in time to his singing. But the emperor himself sourly rejected him, accusing the singer of sounding 'more like a canary', and sending him away empty-handed and dejected. The second singer the emperor seemed to like better, but unfortunately the performance degenerated into a fit of coughing after some high notes. The profuse apologies of the impressionist were insufficient to avoid his being physically propelled down the magnificent steps leading up to the royal palace.

The third and last impresario, a woman, stepped forward and this time the court was transfixed. At the bidding of the emperor this woman could sing as purely and as sweetly as the bird itself, and the fact that this artist seemed to need to keep both hands tucked into her tunic didn't appear to spoil the effect.

But when the emperor offered her the gold sovereign as the reward, the singer removed one of her hands from inside the tunic – and a bird flew out, fluttered around the hall and then perched on a suit of armour, singing and trilling all the while like the nightingale it was.

The emperor was not amused, and the hapless performer was thrown into the palace dungeon on a charge of attempting to defraud the royal exchequer. But the singer protested, even as she was being thrown down the dungeon steps, that the emperor had wanted someone to sound like a nightingale, and the mechanism of how they achieved it was neither here nor there. Clearly, her performance had been the only really authentic one.

Is she a cheat – or just an entrepreneur?

Fundamentally religious problems

Problems 81–88

(raised by an annoying parishioner on a wet Sunday afternoon, with the Vicar)

PARISHIONER: [*Problem 81*] If God made the universe – where was He before he made it?

VICAR: Goodness! That is a wonderful question. Of course, God does not need the universe for Himself, you see . . .

PARISHIONER: If he doesn't need a universe to be somewhere, why bother making it?

VICAR: Ah . . . Another wonderful question. God made our universe out of love, out of goodness. It is His gift . . .

PARISHIONER: [*Problem 82*] If he made the universe out of love for life and goodness, then why is it so rotten??

VICAR: Well . . . you see . . . [mumble] sometimes seems that way . . . [mumble] couldn't make it completely beautiful . . . [coughs] couldn't have every creature happy and content [mumble, mumble] . . .

PARISHIONER: Excuse ME! It doesn't just SEEM that way! Last week the car broke down on the way to the match! Yesterday the dog bit the milkman! Now the dentist says I've got to have a root filling and won't be able to even speak for a week!

VICAR: Well . . . you see . . . [mumble, mumble] . . . mysterious ways . . .

PARISHIONER: Anyway, if God's all powerful, how come the world's not better?

(*Have a tea break here, and give the Vicar a chance to think/pour the tea.*)

PARISHIONER: [*Problem 83*] Do the souls of animals go to Heaven?

VICAR: Ah! Well, I think perhaps, you know, I like animals, but perhaps they are not really . . .

PARISHIONER: [*Problem 84*] If not – what's it like in Heaven anyway?

VICAR: Ah! Well, I am sure some animals will be there. After all, I often think that for all Mr Jones' efforts with the choir, truly the 'dawn chorus' is really the most heavenly sound the Church hears . . . !

PARISHIONER: [*Problem 85*] If some animals are in Heaven – will some animals be in Hell too?

VICAR: No, no, no . . . My Goodness! [chuckle].

(*Pause, while the Vicar eats the best biscuits from the tray.*)

VICAR: You see, the Bible tells us that animals don't have souls. They're just very complicated, very lovely, machines.

PARISHIONER: [*Problem 86*] If that's so, why do we think we're different? What makes us so important?

VICAR: Ah . . . well, we can't talk about interesting things like this with animals, can we?

PARISHIONER: [*Problem 87*] But you could with a computer. In fact, I have done so, and the computer had some very interesting things to say . . . [The Vicar looks a bit put out.] Is there a computer-heaven that the souls of computers will go to?

VICAR: Well, really, I don't think we should take the idea of souls too simplistically . . .

PARISHIONER: [*Problem 88*] Is there just one cosmic soul, then, a universal consciousness . . .

VICAR: Goodness, is that the . . .

PARISHIONER: . . . and if so, what makes us so different from rocks and . . . ?

[General problem: How to get rid of the parishioner]

Problem 89
The evangelist

In a southern US state, a town is racked by continued freak weather including hurricanes and droughts. The local evangelist gives a sermon on WKYTV warning that the problem is too much loose living and bad behaviour. The Reverend Newman suggests that instead, all decent people should come to his church the following Sunday and drink from a special vat of thick, red 'moral cleanser'. But pointing his finger menacingly at the camera, the Rev. warns that any evil person who tries to drink the cleanser will be 'eaten up' inside and die within the month.

The next Sunday, there are queues of thousands of locals, all trying to cleanse themselves. And the next Sunday. And soon, even those who initially mocked the idea, feel obliged to at least show that they are not responsible for any of the township's continuing misfortunes.

About three weeks after the initial broadcast, people start developing a completely unprecedented mystery disease which seems to result in complex destruction of internal tissues, and soon some thirteen citizens are dead. The police department move quickly, arresting Reverend Newman and charging him with homicide. He is found guilty and booked an appointment with the electric chair. But he appeals. On further investigation, it is established that his 'moral cleanser' is simply pure tomato juice, and completely harmless. His attorney points out that the charge is nonsense on two grounds: first, the illness was clearly psychosomatic, caused by perhaps those persons believing themselves to be evil, and this is something the Reverend had not accused them individually of – indeed, he had thanked and blessed everyone who came to his church for the 'cleansing' ceremony. Second, even if the process had had this unfortunate effect, the citizens had undergone it voluntarily.

Is the Reverend guilty?

Elementary problems of natural philosophy

Problem 90
Poincaré's problem

On a far away planet live the gaseous people, let us call them 'the Jeometers', a strange people, yes, but in many respects not so very different from us. To understand the most important difference, you need to know a bit about their planet.

Their planet is made only of gases. At the centre the temperature is very high, and this is where the gaseous people evolved and normally live. At the surface, however, the temperature is very, very low. In fact, it is absolute zero. (The significance of this will become clear later.)

As the Jeometers move around their planet, a small but subtle change takes place. Because of the change in temperature, the further they go from the centre, the smaller they become. And not just them; the smaller all the creatures and all the artefacts of the gaseous planet become. The second important thing is that everything changes at exactly the same rate, so nothing gets out of kilter.

One year, the Jeometers determine they must explore the upper reaches of their planet and construct a massive ladder which they stand upright with its top disappearing far into the clouds. One of the Jeometers' geometers sets off up it, with the task of finding out how far the gaseous planet extends. There is great excitement, but it is dissipated somewhat when the geometer returns a few days later to say the ladder is nowhere near long enough.

For years and years sections of ladder are added, but it seems it is in vain. Each time the geometers return to say that the ladder is still not long enough.

Actually, as they ascend the ladder, both the Jeometers and the ladder itself are shrinking, shrinking so small that it is physically impossible for them to ever get there. (At absolute zero, they will shrink to absolutely nothing.) Yet as they climb up, becoming colder and colder and at the same time smaller and smaller, the steps on the ladder, their measuring rods – everything – are also getting smaller and smaller, so they never realise the shrinking is happening. Eventually, the Jeometers decide their planet is infinitely large. Which it isn't.

The problem is, whose measurements are the 'real ones'?

Problem 91
Problems with the speed of light

In the 1880s two Americans, Albert Michelson and Edward Morley, equipped with nothing more than a large wind-up clock and some mirrors, set about measuring the speed of light. Knowing, as we all do, that speed is relative,* they expected to find a discrepancy between the speed of light coming from the sun with the additional benefit of the earth's spin, and as viewed with the earth's spin whisking the observer in the opposite direction. (And the speed of the earth is considerable. It's only because everything is already moving in harmony with it that we don't normally notice it.) Try as they might, pointing the mirrors this way and that, even using a multi-sided rotating mirror in between to increase the distance the light was measured over and so on, neither Michelson nor Morley could find any significant difference in the measured speed of light. It always seemed to go everywhere at about 300,000km a second.

Was it experimental error? (Should they have used water clocks?)

---

* Two cyclists riding towards each other at 16km an hour will collide with a force equivalent to 32km an hour. That is, if they're not looking.

Problem 92
Further problems of natural philosophy

Here's one you can do for yourself in the garden shed. Point a large, powerful telescope at a bright star and, instead of looking through it, project the single point of starlight onto a piece of card. Rather than a bright dot of light, you will see a bright dot of light surrounded by a bit of blurring. The light has spread out, by the phenomenon known as diffraction, the process seen most easily with waves in liquids. If a wave goes through a 10m gap in a sea wall, it does not carry on as a 10m-wide wave, in an area of calm water, but immediately spreads out. The amount of diffraction with light is very small, and we can normally suppose light to be little parcels of energy that travel in straight lines. But they don't always.

Now take a piece of cardboard and cut a slit in it. You will need a good pair of scissors as the slit must be very fine. About one thousandth of a millimetre would be nice. Now shine a light through the slit onto a screen, preferably using a lightbulb that allows through only one type of light, one colour.

After passing through the slit, the light will spread out a little, again by diffraction. Light, as noted already, is usually thought of as little particles, known as photons, which are shot out by hot things, such as the sun. One good reason to think this is so is that there is a certain minimum amount of light energy which is always detected, or a multiple of this amount. Indeed, if you make your shed very, very dark, and turn your light source down very, very carefully, the image on the screen would cease to be a smooth wash of light but would break up into lots of tiny dots, each dot representing one of these minimum packets of light. But, for comparison, just a standard house lightbulb gives out 100 million million million photons every second! Even so, the eye is actually so sensitive that in total darkness, other things being equal, it can detect a single photon.

So far, so good: we have little packets of light energy being sent in a very rapid stream from our special light source through the slit. Now we make another, parallel, slit a set distance from the first, and observe a peculiar thing. Instead of the light particles taking the opportunity of two equally good ways to get to the screen, to make the screen brighter, *parts of the screen actually go darker*, whilst others become two times or even four times brighter. The light travelling through one slit 'interferes' with the light travelling through the other, and the pattern on the screen (in the area of diffraction) looks like one of wave interference with bands of light and darkness.

So is this an elusive example of something that can be two contradictory things all at once? The something red all over and green all over that philosophers search for? Is light energy (and the same with all the other forms of energy) a stream of separate, tiny particles, or a continuous wave form, or both?

Problem 93

Advanced further problems of natural philosophy

If we turn down our light source from 100 million whatever photons a second to, say, just ten a second, we see the problem, if not the screen, very clearly. These last few photons of light head off, one by one, for the screen, some of them hitting the piece of card but the odd one going through a slit. Now, according to common sense, each should be able to land on the screen unaffected by whether the other slit is there – or not. But none of them, no matter how long we wait, will try to land on the dark areas seen in the interference pattern with lots of light. After all, if an individual photon could behave in this way, it might take a long time but, eventually, the screen would record a picture more like the one-slit experiment with the light diffusing evenly, than the interference one. And the individual photons recognise the contradiction. They continue to behave individually as 'waves' *all on their own*. Points where the light particle could go when just one slit is open become unavailable when the other slit is open. (Incidentally, the same thing, scientists have observed, will happen with any small particle – electrons, whole atoms or even molecules will do just as well.)

In experiments, the individual particles of light seem to know about the other slit on the piece of card, indeed what is going on elsewhere in the universe. For, in principle at least, the distance between the slits can be any size, and the same interference effect will apply. (Although if the slits were even a metre apart, the screen might need to be on the moon before the deflected light begins to converge.)

Suppose we asked our neighbour if we could borrow their particle detector to check whether the light energy is still travelling in 'whole photons', rather than splitting into two and going through both slits and thereby getting in and out of phase with each other. We would find, indeed, that it was still travelling as a whole photon, and that this attempted explanation does not fit with observation. But we would find something else too. The mere act of putting the particle detector next to one slit causes the wavy pattern, the 'interference' effect, to disappear!

But how can a particle know anything anyway?

Problem 94
Schrödinger's cat's problem

The physicist Erwin Schrödinger described, back in 1935, one aspect of this strange phenomenon. He placed his cat in a sealed box with a piece of radioactive material which might or might not send out a sub-atomic particle. If it did, the Geiger counter was designed to trigger a release of poisonous gas in the box, and thereby kill his cat. The Geiger counter was set up to be triggered just enough to give a 50–50 chance of a particle being detected, and therefore the cat an even chance of being poisoned or not. (In those days, this sort of experiment was acceptable, particularly as it was only a thought experiment.)

Radioactive behaviour is unpredictable (except in a general, statistical probability way). There is no way of working out whether or not the Geiger counter will be triggered. If the sub-atomic event does not occur – the cat lives. Otherwise, it dies. Just as the photon (in Problem 93) will quite happily go through both slits until someone tries to measure or detect it, at which point what the physicists call 'the collapse of the wave function' takes place, the particle can both trigger the poison gas and not trigger the poison gas. Until someone looks, Schrödinger's idea is that his cat, for a while, is both alive and dead!

Will Professor Schrödinger's experiment work?

Problem 95

The space yacht's black hole

Mr Megasoft has bought a very expensive yacht. It is a space yacht, designed with a huge (1,000km-wide) solar sail to fly in space. (This works because light actually weighs something. Not very much, although physicists calculate that about 160 tons of sunlight fall on the earth every day.) Using the universal force of light waves, the yacht accelerates steadily away from its moorings in low earth orbit towards the nearest star, at a steady rate of acceleration to produce, as all owners of sports cars know, a feeling of being pressed backwards in the seats. It creates the equivalent of a new spaceship gravity, calculated for Megasoft's comfort, at one 'g', approximately equivalent to that back on earth. In a year, the solar yacht has reached a considerable proportion of the speed of light although, of course, it is unable to exceed that speed. But when Mr Megasoft looks backwards he sees something awful behind him: the stars are going out one by one!

What has happened to the universe?

Pretty final problems

Problem 96
Schopenhauer's problem

Poor Arthur Schopenhauer (1788–1860). Try as he might, he can't really get interested in any of the standard 'problems of philosophy'. All he can think about is sex. So he tries to make it part of his philosophy. 'The genitals are the focus of the will,' he scratches out on his parchment and adds, rather sourly, that love is simply 'the expression of the species' need to reproduce'. It ebbs away as soon as the genetic function has been fulfilled.

Can this possibly be true?

Problem 97
Schopenhauer's problem too

Arthur looks at this and sees that it is good. However, he thinks, it still doesn't really sum up the sensitivity and subtlety of his own case, and he modifies his theory slightly to allow people like himself, Plato and all the Buddhists, to follow an alternative path in which it is possible to transcend this prompting and simply contemplate reality without striving and pain. 'Company', he writes, 'is a fire at which to warm oneself at a distance'.

Is a life of solitary contemplation really better than social companionship – even love?

Problem 98

A fairly terminal problem for dull philosophers

The definition of validity used in standard 'formal logic' is this:

A philosophical argument is valid if it is not possible for the premises (assumptions) to be true and yet the conclusion to be false.

Put in other words, when a problem is expressed in the correct, logical way it can be known for certain that, if all the assumptions as to matters of fact are correct, then, because the problem has been addressed using the rules of logic, we can be *certain* that the conclusion is also true.

Is this a good start for solid, rigorous thinking?

Problem 99
Descartes' big problem

How do I know I'm not in the middle of some awful, *101 Philosophy Problems* nightmare?

A nightmare of unusual proportions, certainly, that goes on and on with remarkable consistency and detail – but a miasma none the less, completely detached from reality? How do I know I haven't fallen into the clutches of a malignant demon, intent on deceiving me?

Or perhaps even a malignant doctor? One who has recovered my brain after some nasty accident (involving too many chip butties and driving no doubt) and is now keeping it suspended in a vat of chemicals as part of a ghastly medical experiment. Feeding it made-up 'sense-data' along coloured wires: purple for hearing, black for touch, yellow for taste, blue for vision . . . ?

Problem 100

The problem of how to get to 101 (unsolved)

There certainly are a lot of philosophy problems. The more you look at it, the more you can find. Problems stretching away as far as the eye can see. And most of them unsolved. It's true that, these days, with powerful computers, telescopes, cranes and so on, we could calculate how heavy the problems would be, if they were all collected together and put in one place. Or how far they would stretch if they were laid end to end. Or we could look very closely at the problems and see exactly what bits they are made up of. Because, these days, computers and technology can do virtually anything, and certainly everything that matters. Except, perhaps, solve philosophy problems.

Because the problem with philosophy problems is that they don't have proper solutions.

Is that a problem with philosophy problems?

Problem 101
The problem of existence

Mr Megasoft has been reading a book on the nature of existence. The book says that the purpose of being alive is simply to pass on your 'genetic material', through sex, and producing children.

There is actually quite a lot of circumstantial evidence for this. First, the sexual drive is very strong, and seems to achieve little other than the production of children. Second, at least amongst some of the population, there is a tendency to look after these children and make sacrifices for them which really cannot be explained any other way than as an investment in their own genetic future. (Certainly not altruism, as few of other people's children arouse the same interest!) This is the 'selfish gene' determining behaviour. And Mr Megasoft thinks it's a very good explanation of why we are alive, and what the point of it all is.

All our other behaviour: football, art, killing other people (and their children) and so on can be explained in this way. And we are even designed to die shortly after the children have grown up and finished with us. It's tidy, even if not very nice.

Mr Megasoft takes his responsibility to pass on his genetic code very seriously. He sets up a secret department in Megasoft Laboratories whose job it is to implant a string of DNA from one of his cells into an unfertilised egg donated by his live-in partner, Charlene. (Tactfully, Mr Megasoft doesn't tell Charlene that the process involves removing her genetic code.) The egg is then deep-frozen and put in a special solar-powered 'escape pod' attached to one of Megasoft's communications satellites. The plan is for the mini-spaceship to be shot off into deep space for all eternity.

Mr Megasoft thinks this will ensure that his genetic code lasts longer than anyone else's and, indeed, makes it unnecessary for the human race to continue.

There's only one problem with the theory, at least as far as solving the problem of existence goes: if our purpose is simply to pass on our genetic code . . .

...what's the genetic code's purpose?

Discussions

Problem 1
The hanging judge

The 'hanging judge' is a slightly different case of the 'All Cretans are liars' type of paradox, which has kept philosophers from Aristotle to Zeno, and back again to Aquinas, busy for countless years. The paradox originated with the ancient Greek philosopher Epimendes, who is supposed to have claimed that people from Crete always told lies. This was not only somewhat racist, but somewhat inexplicable, as he himself was from Crete. If it was true, then what he himself was saying should have been a lie, but if it were a lie, then . . . The truth of the claim affects the circumstances in which it is uttered which affects the truth of the claim, which . . . etc., etc., an infinite twisting and turning of the truth. Effectively, the statements are neither true nor false, although they look like they ought to be. Unlike sentences such as, say, 'Hello, Vicar,' which do not need to be given a 'truth value'.

And what did the prisoner say? 'I will be hanged tomorrow' (or something similar) will suffice to get him off. The Chief Executioner cannot execute him then because, clearly, the relatives could then sue her for wrongful execution arguing that the Philosopher had been telling the truth when he said 'I will be hanged tomorrow.' Likewise, if the Chief Executioner accepted this problem and opted to send the Philosopher to prison, he might well be sent straight back, with the governor lacking the authority to admit him. For the governor would see that the Philosopher has clearly lied to the court again and so the punishment should have been execution after all.

Problem 2
The cow in the field

Many people would say that, given human frailty, it is enough to say that we know something if:

- we believe it to be the case;

- we have a good, relevant reason for our belief;
- and it is so.

This is knowledge as 'justified true belief'.

However, in Farmer Field's case, he satisfies all these conditions, and yet we still might feel he did not really know that Daisy was in the field.

This problem is also set out in Plato's *Theaetetus* (201c–210d), and, in slightly more formal language, has perplexed many philosophers ever since, particularly since the twentieth-century interest in 'analytic' philosophy. In this example, Farmer Field:

- believed the cow was safe;
- had evidence that this was so (his belief was justified);
- and it was true that his cow was safe.

However, we might still feel he didn't really 'know' it. What this all suggests is that a different definition of 'knowledge' is needed. Although all knowledge may have to be 'true, justified beliefs', not all true, justified beliefs seem to be knowledge. Many philosophers would say that what is needed is a more *complicated* (!) account – to get around this sort of counter-example.

This rejection of the three conditions as jointly still 'insufficient'* encouraged a few philosophers to simply add an extra rule: nothing inferred from a false belief counts as knowledge. But this is, of course, a bit tautological, tautology being the last refuge of the philosopher.

Other philosophers have tried to dispense with the first requirement, allowing someone to know without necessarily believing, whilst others wished to make the criterion for 'knowing' to be something more than just belief, suggesting instead that what is required is 'acceptance', whatever that is . . .

The problem of how to find rock-bottom certainty is the underlying theme of much Western philosophy, as practised by the ancient Greeks and epitomised by René Descartes (see Problem 99) in his questions to himself whilst meditating in his

---

*More recently by E. L. Gettier in a suitably short article in *Analysis*.

sixteenth-century oven room. He thought he'd found the answer in the certainty of his own existence as a thinking being, famously encapsulated as *Cogito ergo sum* – I think therefore I am. This, René believed, was something that he definitely did know – not just believed to be the case.

Problem 3
Protagoras' problem

It is said that the court was so puzzled that it adjourned for 100 years. The paradox is that both ways of thinking seem to be correct, but they lead to two opposing conclusions.

This is a 'classic' problem – indeed a classical problem – such as the ancient Greeks liked to discuss. It's not a 'trick' – or if there is one, no one has discovered it yet. Neither Euathlos nor Protagoras can be faulted on their logic – but both of them can't be right. Which tends to undermine logic, and with it the basis for most of our reasoning. Which is why the Ancients considered these problems so interesting.

M' learned friend adds:

Lawyers have also been very interested in the paradox, even if it never reached the celebrated Court of Areopagus, which was probably too busy trying animals and inanimate objects for murder. In part, this is because many bits of legal jargon refer to themselves, for example, saying things like 'this law is no longer valid', or even 'this book is copyright' (it is, but only by virtue of containing the announcement itself). Then again, there are many complicated legal 'circles' such as occur occasionally with insurance policies which attempt to exclude losses 'covered by other policies'.

In the Ohio *State versus Jones* case in 1946, Protagoras' problem was specifically cited in evidence. Dr Jones was being accused of carrying out an illegal operation on a Ms Harris. The case relied crucially on Ms Harris' testimony that she had asked him to carry out the operation, and that he had then done so. The problem for the judge was that if Dr Jones had carried out an illegal operation, then Ms Harris was an accomplice, and her evidence was suspect, and legally unsound. In this case, both the lower court judge and the Court of Appeals allowed the matter to be decided (illogically if necessary) by a jury. These non-philosophers simply ignored the cunning circularity and found the devious Dr Jones guilty.

117

Problem 4
The hairdresser of Hindu Kush

The alarming thought that occurs to the hairdresser is, what is he to do about his own hair? Whatever he does, he seems to break one or other of the rules.

The 'Barber' paradox, as this is more usually known, is a version of a very old paradox that has come to the fore ever since the philosopher Bertrand Russell came across it in the early years of the twentieth century. Russell rather inelegantly summed it up as the problem of the 'set of all sets that are not members of themselves – is it a member of itself?' He was so appalled at the implications of the paradox, not only for logic, but for mathematics and even ordinary language, that he wrote in his autobiography that his life's work seemed dashed to pieces, and for weeks he could scarcely eat or sleep. He sent the paradox to his co-worker, the mathematical philosopher Göttlob Frege, who commented, 'arithmetic trembles'.

A number of solutions have been suggested. One is that the hairdresser should try to outwit the guards with a bit of clever argument, and another is that the hairdresser should arrange a nasty shock for himself with the aim of making all his hair fall out. However, neither of these devices really gets to grips with the fundamental problem.

In his *Principia Mathematica* Bertrand Russell undertook to find solutions to no less than seven incarnations of the paradox, and worked on his reformulation thus: Is the set of all sets that are not members of itself a member of itself, or is it not, and if it is not, is it? Admirably precise though this specification of the problem is, it does not actually help resolve the contradiction, and Russell took the drastic step of saying that all statements which refer to themselves should be 'outlawed', or at least treated as meaningless. Unfortunately, a great many meaningful statements are self-referential – arguably, that is what makes them meaningful.

Problem 5
The raven

Or even if the effect is more permanent and the raven stays green? But everything not black is not a raven . . .

The problem could be posed as 'all swans are white', which was thought to be equally true, until, of course, black swans were discovered alive and well in

Australia. Which just goes to show that even a dire issue like this can have some bearing on reality. To avoid this sort of rude intrusion happening again, many philosophers prefer to discuss whether all bachelors are unmarried men, whether 2 + 2 = 4, or whether water needs to be composed of molecules of one oxygen and two hydrogen (see Problems 60–71). The discussion can then centre on whether the terms are analytic or synthetic, true *a priori* or *a posteriori** and so on, and scientists can be left to their tentative, empirical study of the world. The Court Philosopher in this way may be trying to turn an 'inductive' question into a 'conceptual' one. But what about the green raven? It is probably – *a posteriori* – a synthetic raven. (Nearest thing to a philosophical joke . . .)

Problem 6
The tuck-shop dilemma

Jane will be thinking that if she does not confess, and nor does Janet, they will both have to be let off by Dr Gibb. However, if she does not confess and Janet does, then she will be expelled! Perhaps, then, the safest thing to do is to admit to stealing from the tuck-shop and be suspended for the rest of the term.

This, in fact, is the way guilty people do reason when put in similar situations. As long as they cannot communicate with their accomplices, and thus promise each other to keep 'mum', prisoners will mitigate their losses by confessing – even though the best solution requires them not to. (Of course, *innocent* people may adopt a course of action which is totally irrational and causes them much more bother than confessing would have done.)

The first time this problem was set out was in 1951 by Merrill Flood in America, and since then 'The prisoner's dilemma' has spawned wide discussion of the nature of 'rationality' and a new study, 'Game theory'. This looks, for instance, at what is likely to happen in a situation like a global nuclear arms race, where both players are better off if neither upgrades their weapons, and the worst situation is if you don't and the other side does. As in the problem, recent history shows the middle option prevails – both sides spend all their money on upgrading their weapons without

* These terms are introduced here in the spirit they were invented – solely in order to confuse the reader.

getting any military advantage. At least, until the element of communication is introduced, at which point trust can blunt the horns of the dilemma.

Problem 7

The unexpected exam

A bit like Zeno's classic 'Achilles and the tortoise' paradox, there is no flaw in Bob's reasoning, but it doesn't work. Each step of the argument Patricia put is correct, and so is the conclusion – but, unfortunately for classes everywhere, it just doesn't match reality!

Problem 8
Sorites

The question is, which of the three ships is the original *Thunderprow*? The material one, on the trestles, the one being used – or the mental one in the mind of the designer? Or is it another?

This is the same problem facing someone trying to identify how many grains of sand make a 'heap', although it also raises questions about 'identity', whatever that is! You might think this easy, at least to estimate, but try adding one grain to another and it is clear that the distinction is unreliable. (And imagine you get punished if you add unnecessary extra grains of sand to the heap!) Humans specialise in 'fuzzy thinking' whereby we put together inadequate information to come to a conclusion. But when it comes to reasoning, even humans rely on one iron distinction – that between what is and what is not. So, if it is impossible to say how many 10p's make a beggar rich, or how many grains of sand make a sandpit, it is also impossible to say when blue is not green, when an inch is really an inch, and so on. It's worse than saying all our reasoning relies on approximations – because what are the approximations being compared to?

Problem 9
The Society for Useless Information's problem

The problem is that no matter how useless the information brought by applicants appears to be, and some of it is very useless, including lots of disbanded tiers of local government regulations, or torn out pages from second order logic textbooks (indeed, even the whole textbooks) and so on, if it entitles the person producing it to join the esteemed society, then it is not entirely useless after all!

(Attributed originally to Brenda Almond.)

Problem 10
A problem with lentils

So what? The answer is that you should avoid politicians. And it is 'valid'.

Lewis Carroll liked to couch everyday-seeming discussions as a series of vaguely mathematical, vaguely logical statements, all of which actually lead onto each other, and can be used to reach an eventual conclusion, if, that is, we want to reach it.

For starters, in our lentil eaters dilemma, if you take the claim that

everyone in the world has an interest in saving it

and add to it the fact that

nobody interested in saving the world could possibly fail to eat lentils at least once a week

then in the best (albeit indigestible) style of propositional logic you can conclude:

everyone should eat lentils at least once a week

The rest of it is more complicated and to be honest, I gave up (got lost). But apparently it does work.

A logician adds:

EVERYONE should eat lentils AND we know all lentil eaters are meat eaters THEREFORE everyone is a closet carnivore and everyone who is A CLOSET CARNIVORE has psychological problems so everyone seems to eat a lot and SINCE everyone is part of the ecosystem AND all my friends are

NECESSARILY AND NOT CONTINGENTLY drawn from the group of 'everyone in the world' therefore . . .THEREFORE, er . . . all my friends (without wishing to ASSUME the existence of any) . . . are part of the ecosystem . . . AND certainly people with psychological problems are not my friends so IT FOLLOWS that politicians are NOT going to be my friends and THAT THEREFORE I do not like politicians . . .

Which is why I avoid them!

Problem 11
The sentence

Philosophers since (at least) ancient Greece and the 'Liar' paradox have been perplexed and worried by this problem which, stated most simply, goes 'All Cretans are liars', with the problem occurring when this is being said by a native of Crete. Actually, some philosophers say, this is not much of a problem at all, as the Cretan may just be lying. Some Cretans are liars. (Notably me.) (But suppose all other Cretans are liars? The truth uttered by the speaker undoes the claim. If, in fact, lots of Cretans tell the truth occasionally, then it is not, even to the Greeks, a very interesting story. Although what would happen if, in fact, there were only one Cretan in the world – the speaker? Then it would be like the paradoxical version which goes 'I always lie'.)

The Cretan's words are reminiscent of the old Chinese sage's advice to listen carefully to what people tell you, and then think the opposite – then you won't be fooled. The advantage of this variation is that, taken as a general policy, it can even be applied to the advice itself. Which becomes (when listening to the sage), you should always believe and follow what people tell you, in this case, to disbelieve everyone.

(See also the discussion of Problems 1 and 13.)

Problem 12
Diktatia

It seemed a very sensible arraignment, for everyone except the unlucky two, at least until the next bomb went off – at which point the others were all rounded up again. One of the group now suggested that the only morally correct thing to do is to have nothing to do with the execution decision. They should all proclaim their innocence, the wickedness of the government, etc. and then, if they die, it will at least be with clean hands. Better than to again allow two innocents, whether picked by straws, or whether 'volunteers', to die to save their skins! That would be to participate in something quite wrong.

Naturally, not all of the group agree. So someone says they should move to a vote – because that is the only fair way to solve such tricky dilemmas. But is that ethical?

This sort of issue does arise in the real world, most notoriously with the Nazis, who used to round up citizens following resistance attacks and make similar announcements. Some see it as all a matter of mathematics – the choice being all thirty die, or all but two live. But others say that even on the mathematics, the answer is not clear. By giving the government the veneer of legality in selecting its victims they are contributing to future injustices with incalculable costs. And others will say it is wrong to offer up victims whatever the outcomes and calculations.

Problem 13
A relative problem

The issue of 'relativism' dogs all and any attempts to define right and wrong. Marx famously derided all moralities as merely the products of the false consciousness spawned by the ruling classes – before making an impassioned denunciation of the wickedness of capitalism!

The Greeks also recognised the problem. It is discussed by Plato in *The Republic*, where Socrates has one of his more vicious arguments with Thrasymachus, who insists that justice is merely whatever is in the interests of the strongest, rather than Socrates' own rather soppy (idealistic, anyway) view about it. Elsewhere Socrates deals with Protagoras' view that 'Man is the measure of all things'. This comfortable position means, as Aristotle describes in his *Metaphysics*:

> that which seems to exist for each man assuredly does so . . . it follows that the same thing both is and is not, and is both bad and good, and that all other opposite statements are true, because often some particular thing appears

beautiful to some and ugly to others, and that which appears to each man is the measure.

But despite Socrates' efforts, Thrasymachus and Protagoras have many modern-day adherents, and anthropologists regularly dabble in 'cultural relativism'. Certainly, the extent to which our notion of right and wrong depends on social factors and conditioning cannot be underestimated.

One of the great sages of Chinese philosophy, Chang Tzu, used the example of killing to illustrate the relativity of moral judgements. If, as some sages said, killing was wrong, was it wrong to kill a hare when it was the only way to save yourself from starving? Surely not. Perhaps then it was always wrong to kill another human being? But what if that human being was a robber intent on killing and robbing a family? Surely it would then not be wrong to kill him, if that would be the only way to stop him?

All moral knowledge depends in this way on context and situations – it is relative. Chang goes on to prove that in fact all knowledge – not just moral or aesthetic judgements – is equally rooted in context, and equally 'relative'. He puts it in this perfectly inscrutable way:

> Once I, Chuang Chou, dreamed I was a butterfly and was happy as a butterfly. I was conscious that I was quite pleased with myself, but I did not know that I was Chou. Suddenly I awoke, and there I was, visibly Chou. I do not know whether it was Chou dreaming he was a butterfly, or the butterfly dreaming it was Chou.

His conclusion (like Schopenhauer's, see Problems 96 and 97) is that we should strive to transcend the world of such distinctions.

Problems 14–15
The dog and the professor, I and II

With hindsight, we may feel the answer to the original problem to be clear enough. But without hindsight, we would need to decide whether the Professor had an absolute duty to save the life of a dog – or not. If it was an absolute duty, then clearly he would have to rescue it even if he was not rushing to give a lecture, but was a surgeon on his way to perform a life-saving operation. This we might find hard to accept.

If it is not an absolute duty, then maybe not the third week, but the fourth or the fifth week of the Professor wading in to rescue the animal would have the college director, if not the students, getting a bit restive at the calculation of duties.

However, arguably, Prof. Purple is missing out on the important emotive aspect of all decision-making, and the fact that this is neither regular nor predictable nor consistent, as no doubt he would complain, does not mean that it is not important. David Hume, the eighteenth-century philosopher, tried to make the notion of 'sympathy' the keystone of his moral theory, before abandoning the attempt to make morality scientific. He recognised this in his observation that 'an *is* does not imply an *ought*', to the effect that, sooner or later, we all fall back on our feelings in order to make any choices.

Problems 16–17
Problems in the Lost Kingdom of Marjon, I and II

Various ethical assumptions are lurking in the Marjonian debate. There is the hidden assumption, perhaps based on some notional 'rights', that there is something wrong with some people having too much whilst others have too little! Such an assumption flies in the face of practical politics. In any case, less cynically, it may be, as the Chair of the Community Council says, in the interests of the majority, both rich and poor, to have a system with incentives. It may be that the dissidents' calculation of the benefits of redistribution are short-term and illusory. And the 'right' of the poor not to go hungry is shrewdly set against the 'right' of all not to have their freedom diminished.

The Marjonians are grappling with the problem faced by all forms of social organisation: what seems perfectly acceptable when things are going well becomes quite unacceptable, despotic even, when things are not. It is in difficult times that the duty of the governed to be governed is tested.

The idea that there is such a duty is a convenient fiction, encapsulated in the imaginary 'social contract' of philosophers such as Thomas Hobbes. It was Hobbes who pointed out that 'in the state of nature', there is no law, and no distinction between right and wrong. But then, life in the state of nature was 'nasty, brutish and short'. So Hobbes, who lived through the English Civil War, thought it was better to surrender the right to decide for yourself what was in your interests and if necessary live under a dictator, than allow challenges to authority. For the harm made possible by dictators (he thought) was limited in scope, compared to the chaos of anarchic society. On the other hand, as John Locke – generally credited as the author of the principles of the American Constitution – was to write a century later, for many people the social contract is worse than the state of nature it is supposed to save them from, because of the arbitrary powers it gives to the sovereign. Who, Locke asked, would sign a contract to escape from 'polecats and foxes', if the result was to be put 'at the mercy of lions'?

Historically and socially, the economic success of liberal democracy, with its 'unnatural' assumption of the equal merit of all citizens, has led to the idea of there being inalienable human political rights gradually but steadily gaining acceptance.

Problems 18–20
The Lost Kingdom and the pesky-fly problem, I, II and III

A few weeks later, many of those who chewed the leaves have died, including the one who spoke out at the meeting, but the majority of the Marjonians are saved from the disease. On a conventional 'utilitarian' calculation, that should make it all right, but some people will have niggling doubts . . .

The issues here, as with many ethical problems, are intertwined in a complicated sort of way, but what the contemporary American philosopher, John Rawls, has pointed out is that, in order to make a fair and 'rational' decision, the people deciding must not be allowed to have a partisan interest. For example, the question of whether to irrigate the island can be approached objectively, by an outsider, on the basis of what would benefit the most people (which is the principle of utilitarianism) whilst also bearing in mind the issues of individual freedom and liberty. Much the most difficult part of the pesky-fly debate concerns the knowledge which some people have that they personally will be worse off by being immunised than they would be by risking getting the disease again. If they only knew that they had a two-thirds chance of dying of the disease and a one-twentieth chance of dying from the tabako leaves, then a simple mathematical calculation enables everyone to agree on the immunisation programme. However, if we do know the identity of those who will survive the disease, it is in many ways 'unethical' to expose them to a risky procedure which has very little advantage for them. The only possible way out of this for the Marjonians might be to recognise that even for someone with natural immunity to the disease, it is worth taking quite a high risk to help others – amongst whom might be included their own family and friends.

Unfortunately, these dilemmas can be all too real. Recently, some scientists have proposed treating AIDS – a frequently fatal disease of the immune system that affects large numbers of people, for example, in sub-Saharan Africa – with country-wide vaccination programmes. These would offer up to 90 per cent protection against the disease, at the price of giving the disease to between 1 and 10 per cent of the population of the country . . . On one calculation, the disease could be eradicated in fifty years, using the vaccination, although treatment would raise the sort of philosophical issues in the problem. Then there are also more straightforward concerns. On one computer model of the effects, the entire population itself is wiped out, as the vaccine itself becomes slowly fatal.

These problems may apply in schools where immunisation programmes are carried out which carry a small risk to individual children, whilst offering general benefits to the school community.

Problems 21–23
New Diktatia, I, II and III

Truth is stranger than fiction . . .

Problem 24
The bent coin problem

Matt must be right. Any time a coin is tossed, there is a 50–50 chance of it coming up heads or tails. (A 'fair' coin.) We can measure this by experiments – simply tossing a coin a thousand times and watching to see if the number of heads and tails is about 500–500 – or something else. But nothing 'makes' the coin come up tails – even a previous long run of coming up heads. The more times we toss the coin, the more the proportions seem to settle down to this. But they don't have to –

unless we toss the coin an infinite number of times. The problem for Louie is that the coin is not bent at all – just that, although we think twenty heads one after the other is unlikely, the universe is indifferent to the pattern.

Tom Stoppard describes the battle of Rosencrantz and Guildenstern over the tossing of coins – ninety times it comes up heads (in the play *Rosencrantz and Guildenstern are Dead*, 1966). It does seem unlikely, but then suppose, like Louie, Guildenstern changes his call every so often – and yet keeps consistently losing. Is that any less 'unlikely'? (This psychological prejudice is sometimes known as the 'gamblers' fallacy'.)

Does it matter? Well, it might. If, for example, a nuclear reactor is safe except if a series of rare events happens, we tend to multiply the probabilities together (they are measured in fractions) – of a spanner falling in the reactor core, of the warning system failing, of the back-up warning system being turned off, of the staff being asleep – to come out with a very, very low probability, like 'one in a thousand million'. But, unlike the coins, we cannot repeat the situation indefinitely until the statistical probabilities balance out. In some sense, a one in a thousand million outcome is as likely as any of the other individual thousand million possibilities to be the next one along!

If you're not convinced, consider the statistical odds of a well-shuffled pack of cards being dealt out to four whist players (the game where one suit is trumps, and you try to win 'tricks') and each player ending up with all the cards of just one suit. It's actually very unlikely: about a one in 2,235,197,406,895,366,368,301,600,000 chance according to a calculation made in 1939 by Horace Norton of University College London. How unlikely is that? Well, put another way, if everyone in the world, say that is about a billion people, played an enthusiastic 100 games a day, every day of the year, *for a million years*, the odds against it are still a hundred to one. Yet, more than one time, such hands have been dealt. One such case involved the pensioners of the Bucklesham Village Whist Club who, in January 1998, were highly amused when (after Mrs Hazel Ruffles, 64, had given the cards a good shuffle) one of the players announced they had thirteen trumps. They were then increasingly amazed as each of the players discovered they too had complete hands of just one suit, as of course did the 'dummy' hand, face down on the table.

The moral is, if you live near a nuclear power station, consider moving.

Well, according to the Principle of Insufficient Reason, the odds are 50–50.

A bit more on probability theory

There are various ways to work out the probability or likelihood of something happening. The obvious way is to work out all the possible outcomes, say, of picking a card at random from a pack, and divide it by the number of successful ones. With the cards there are fifty-two possible outcomes (leaving the jokers out) and the chance of it being the ace of hearts is, therefore, one in fifty-two. The chance of getting any ace is one in thirteen. Because all the cards are equally likely to be picked, this simple approach works.

On the other hand, if we are mischievously named 'Englebert-Laughing-dog-Pumpkinface' by our parents (and doubtless some people are) and we attend a school of 1,000 other people, we are, at the least, *unlikely* to find anyone else sharing our first name, even if there is a general statistical rule about first names that, in a group of 1,000 people, it is to be expected. This knowledge of what is 'likely' and 'unlikely' in the first place is what Dr Wellie is getting at when he says that, in the absence of any information, we should assume there are only two equally likely possibilities – something either is, or it isn't.

Funnily enough, using this sort of mathematical approach, it can be seen that whenever two football teams (plus the referee) are on the pitch, the likelihood of players having at least one pair of shared birthdays between them is also about 50–50. This can be used as a 'party-trick' to impress non-mathematicians, as the apparently strange coincidence of people sharing the same birthday in a relatively small group (compared to the number of days in the year) can actually be fairly confidently predicted once the group gets over about thirty people.

Out of all the things that happen, statistically we *might* expect at least some of them to appear very odd. And this certainly does seem to be the case.

Take the odds of being hit by a train on a level crossing. They are thankfully low. But there are several bizarre and unfortunate cases like the following. In Italy in 1991, a young lady was killed by a train on a level crossing. Four years later, her father was also run over by a train. On the *same* level crossing, at the *same* time and by the *same* train driver.

More historically, in 1833, the novelist Edgar Allan Poe wrote a novel which described three starving shipwrecked sailors who only survive by eating the cabin boy, imaginatively dubbed 'Richard Parker'. Fifty-one years later, three shipwrecked sailors were actually rescued. They had only survived by eating the cabin boy. *The name of the unfortunate boy was Richard Parker.*

On a (slightly) more positive note, there are various true stories such as that of the worried parents during the war, who dialled their daughter to warn her against using the bomb shelter. They dialled the wrong number and got a stranger instead, who was just on their way out. Whilst on the telephone a bomb landed outside, just where the stranger would have been – had it not been for the fortuitous wrong number.

Finally, there are well-documented cases like that of the nervous traveller who, on checking his lucky elephant mascot before flying, found it had been crushed in his bag. The traveller immediately abandoned his travel plans and refused to board the flight. The plane took off – and crashed with no survivors.

And if you're really interested . . .

Pierre Simon Laplace, who set out his logical theories of the subject in 'Essai philosophique sur les probabilites' (1814), once said that the most important questions in life were those involving calculations of probability. And probability certainly has had an important role in philosophy. After all, it involves consideration of some favourite problems: the future, notably the gruebleen assumption that it will resemble the past; knowledge; the laws of nature and so on.

Kant was interested in distinguishing between things that were 'empirically' possible and 'logically' possible, whilst Descartes was more inclined towards what could be imagined as 'possible', which is a kind of psychological possibility. Aristotle was particularly interested in 'potentiality', which he summed up with his example of a block of marble which he thought might have the 'potential' to become a statue of Hermes. Aristotle also compared a builder who builds to one who does not, a sleeping man to an awake one and a man who sees to one who 'has sight but whose eyes are shut' saying that all these examples highlight the difference between 'potentiality' and 'actuality'.

To say something is 'probable' is to put it somewhere between 'possible' and absolutely certain. Although the Stoics, and Hobbes too, thought that if something was possible, then that meant it had to happen, as otherwise it was not really 'possible' (which is another take on the nuclear power station). On this basis, it is right to talk of things in the measurable world being 'possible', but not of things in the logical world being 'possible', and hence it is (some philosophers say) misleading to say that logic can deal with probability. (Sorry, this is probably beginning to confuse you.) Similarly, mathematical theories of probability superimpose a 'grid of certainty' upon the 'partially unstructured' – upon the comparative judgements of likelihood of naive common sense. Nothing in the mathematical theory of probability can settle the proper 'values' of possibilities. (Which was Louie's problem in the bent coin problem.) 'Logical theory has to explain how *a priori* truths can have any bearing on the practical problem of anticipating the unknown on the basis of non-demonstrable reasons', wrote Locke as part of a look at probability in the *Essay Concerning Human Understanding*. Frequency calculations, as taught in maths class, fall apart with situations which only occur occasionally from out of a range of possibilities.

Problem 26
The infinite hotel

Although the notion of infinity does not strictly allow you to add one or multiply it by two, the Advertising Standards Council rules against Zake, saying that Harry's infinite list of rooms is longer than Zake's, as can be seen if one merely remembers that the list of rooms with bathrooms (which is every twelfth room) is also infinitely long, but clearly there are more rooms without bathrooms than with them. Indeed, the number of taps in the infinite hotel is larger than the number of rooms, there being a washbasin, shower and bidet in each room, without even counting the taps on the baths.

A mathematical expert adds:

Intuitively, many people would think (like the Advertising Council) that an infinite hotel with rooms 1a, 1b, 2a, 2b, 3a, etc. must have more rooms than an infinite hotel with just rooms 1, 2, 3, . . . But as Zake's experts unsuccessfully argue, following up work in the nineteenth century by the philosopher Georg Cantor, if in fact, Zake went to Harry's hotel and renamed room 1a, '1', and room 1b, '2', room

2a, '3' and so on, the hotels would appear exactly the same again! *And* Harry's rooms would be smaller.

Georg Cantor specialised in infinity, and towards the last years of the nineteenth century proved that there were several kinds of infinity. There were 'countable' infinities, which means any collection, like the bedrooms or the number of taps in the infinite hotel, in our hotel, which can be counted using ordinary (natural) numbers, 1, 2, 3, etc. . . . Then there were uncountable collections, such as the number of points on a line or what mathematicians call 'real numbers' – the infinity of numbers lying between 1 and 2, for example. These 'uncountable' collections could be said to be bigger than the 'countable' ones, just because. But there are some strange rather counter-intuitive properties of uncountable collections. For example, if you have two lines, one twice as long as the other, they still contain the same number of points. Perhaps, if you have two infinite hotels, together they both contain only the same number of beds as if there were only one. In which case Harry's hotel would not only be smaller (in that the rooms are smaller) but really rather redundant.

(See also the discussion of Zeno's paradoxes below and 'the line point', page 137.)

Problems 27–30
Zeno's paradoxes

Zeno was an ancient Greek philosopher, even more ancient in fact than Aristotle and Plato, the latter of whom puts some of Zeno's arguments into the mouth of Socrates in his fourth-century BC accounts of philosophical debates.

Like many of the ancient Greeks, Zeno of Elea (a small Greek colony seventy miles from Naples) was perplexed by apparent 'contradictions' in the way we understand the world.

The 'Eleatics' subscribed to the notion that the sensory world was illusory, and opposed to a 'real' world that was permanent and unchanging. Zeno himself was a follower of Parmenides, who thought the universe was one and indivisible – an anti-commonsensical view that people sneered at then, and still do. So Zeno's paradoxes were intended to show that if we start from our commonsense view of the world, using our most scrupulous rules of thinking, we none the less end up at equally unsatisfactory conclusions.

If time is a continuous stream there can be no present, yet if time is discontinuous, a series of moments, then there can be only the present (and so no change). Similarly, if space is a smooth continuum there can be no 'here', and if space is 'discontinuous', then there is only here – and hence no motion!

Zeno's concerns here are first to show that the assumption that the world is made up of 'things' to be distinguished from other 'things' – even that most basic notion of things, atoms – can only be made at the expense of having to accept some unacceptable conclusions. For if we divide the world up into bits, we end up with it being impossible for any object to travel any distance at all, however fast (like Achilles or the hare, as this story is sometimes represented*) it may move. And also that however slowly something moves, it somehow manages to travel an infinite distance.

Zeno's activities are only known through scraps of writing – mainly by other people. However, Zeno is also known to have discussed the question of whether an arrow can be said to 'get stuck' during its flight, suggesting that at any particular time, or instant, the arrow is in one particular place, and that if a stretch of time is composed of instants, then it must actually be at rest. Another way of thinking about this is to visualise a billiard ball 'hitting' another. Do they actually share the same space? And if not, how is it that the motion of one can be transferred to the other? To which some philosophers have responded: 'Aha! But the arrow is occupying a different space at each instant!' Which doesn't really seem to address Zeno's point.

In fact Zeno's paradoxes of motion have been refuted by philosophers for over 2,000 years now, with the present crop of scientific/mathematical expert explanations no exception.* However, they have survived because actually, no one can explain them away. Inasmuch as mathematics offers solutions to the problems, it is because mathematics loftily disdains any reference to motion and time in its foundations and ceases to be rooted in the world. (Or as Einstein once wrote, in a paper entitled 'Geometry and Experience': 'as far as the propositions of mathematics refer to reality, they are not certain; and as far as they are certain, they do not refer to reality'.) For example, in maths, we can add the infinite series of one half plus one quarter plus one eighth plus . . . to get just one. And it seems to work. But the

---

* Sometimes even with the hare falling asleep under a tree, which adds unnecessary complication!

* Feebly, modern maths claims the arrow does indeed not move at any instant, but is 'at the appropriate place' at each and every instant and hence appears to move.

conclusion remains based on mathematical conventions. (Even Kurt Gödel, following up Bertrand Russell's hapless attempts to establish arithmetic on firm foundations, was unable to prove everything – instead he settled for a 'Theory of Incompleteness', proving that you can't prove everything.)

The central issue remains whether reality is a continuum of infinitely small instants, or a series of discrete moments. In either case, as Zeno showed, there are problems: Achilles cannot catch the tortoise, and the arrow is motionless at each and every moment of its flight, and should fall to earth stunned at the realisation.

Problem 28
Lost in Space

Discussions

Space is not much discussed in philosophy these days. But its character used to be one of the central debates amongst the Ancients. Democritus said simply the void was what 'was not', Aristotle that it was only a feature to be inferred from the presence of real objects, notably the Earth, and Descartes, contrariwise, that Space itself was a real object, indeed a form of matter, only without any of the usual attributes such as being solid, or anything. Plato it was who had the definitive word on this, as on so many other matters, saying that Space was a very special kind of thing, neither made of matter like the rest of the Universe, nor yet entirely abstract, like the 'Forms' themselves. It was something in between: 'an invisible and characterless thing, that receives all things and shares in a perplexing way all that is intelligible', as Socrates' friend, Timaeus, explains in the dialogue of the same name. So, Problem 28, discussed by Zeno in more abstract form, along with a puzzle to do with how everything made up of parts must either be infinitely small or infinitely large, raises some fundamental issues in physics, not just astronomy. For Newton and Descartes, Space is infinite and unbounded, whilst for Einstein it is finite but still unbounded – strange sounding, but actually something which is possible for any sphere.

Funnily enough this all goes back to another early philosophical thought experiment. Lucretius' 'spear' is a real wood and metal spear, which he carries* (and this is the difficult part) to the very edge of the Universe. Then, with a big hurl, he tosses it over the boundary and into the infinity beyond.

* In *De Rerum Natura*.

What do you suppose happened next? Lucretius asks. And there are only two possibilities. Either the spear crosses the boundary and carries on (even if it then disappears), in which case the boundary is not truly the edge of the universe at all. And if the spear cannot cross, but bounces off some sort of invisible force field or the like, then the line we *thought* was the edge of the Universe is not the true boundary at all, and the spear has yet to cross it. And the wall at the edge of the Universe itself might be infinite. Einstein points out that whatever Kant would have liked, Space does not have to obey the rules of geometry.

Zeno, and the view taken on Space, threaten not only Euclid's useful but still only human-made geometry, but also the basis of the laws of motion, and even the pope. (Descartes even modified his account of the paradoxes to avoid being called to Rome over it, as his friend Galileo was.) Ultimately geometry is still only a mathematical system determined by the assumptions made in setting it up. Whether the system is right for describing the Universe still requires fallible observation. The sum of the angles of a triangle may even, some day, be proved other than 180 degrees, but this possibility can never be proved by measurement.

Does this really matter? Well, maybe not to you or me. But if there are any immortal souls in the Universe, non-material like Space, but still part of it, they might be affected. For astronomers think that ultimately the future of the Universe is expected to be determined by whatever the actual geometry is. Some say if the geometry is 'hyperbolic', the Universe will expand for ever. If the geometry is Euclidian, the Universe will expand at escape velocity. But if the geometry is 'elliptic', the expansion will slow and grind to a halt before the Universe will start to shrink, eventually collapsing in on itself, before perhaps exploding again.

However, the age of the Universe is a bit of a problem, too. It would seem obvious that either the Universe had a beginning – or it didn't. The trouble with it having a beginning is that something must have come of nothing, and what is nothing without something anyway? (The sound of one hand clapping?) On the other hand, if the Universe has always existed, then it must be infinitely old – and that means it's getting older than that infinitely old every minute – which is not really very logical either.

This was the first of Immanuel Kant's four 'Antimonies' or contradictions. As well as inventing new, important-sounding words for philosophers to baffle one another with (see Problems 69–71), Kant followed Zeno and other philosophers by giving examples of how our normal thinking processes can lead us astray.

Problem 29
Dancing in the stadium

By the time they are all in formation, the Texas Belles will have passed twice as many of the High School Hippies, as they have of the Kansas Kats. Therefore, Zeno reasons, it should take twice as long. In fact, the time which the Belles and the Hippies take to reach their place in the formation is the same. Therefore . . . a problem with timings.

Our 'cheerleaders' illustrate the rather elaborate issue of whether 'rows of bodies' can fault the laws of physics by moving at different speeds relative to one another. But it is also more than this.

If lines are made up of discrete (clearly separate) bits – points, or 'units', or even dancing girls – and time is likewise a series of discrete instants, then the only way to measure motion is to count the number of units, or girls (or cats-per-hippy) each girl or unit passes. Or consider the notion that when a line is made up of an infinite number of points, as Euclid said all lines are, implausibly enough, they must either be made up of just one point, which doesn't sound like much of a line – or the same number. (Hopefully this is explained in Figure 1, 'The line point'.) Then either these points must have some length themselves, or they don't – they must be of zero length. If the first, then, no matter how tiny the size, all lines would end up being infinitely long.

On the other hand, if it is the latter, then even an infinite number of zeros would appear to not add up to very much at all. The only way for philosophers around this is to make 'length' independent of the number of points on the line. Which means that any two points in the universe can be one millimetre or one light year apart without it making any difference at least to how many points lie in between.

The 'rows of bodies' are an attempt, as with the other paradoxes, to show the 'absurd' consequences of some of our most basic assumptions about the universe. From Zeno's paradoxes sprang insights into the nature of space time and infinity. In order to cope with the paradoxes, modern science and mathematics needed to develop new conceptual tools in order to progress.

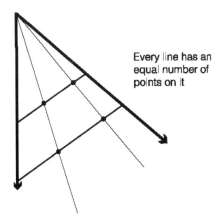

Every line has an
equal number of
points on it

Figure 1   The line point

Problem 31
Fakes and forgeries

The picture obviously has remained the same – but we are asked to accept that the
artist's intentions in painting it are not mere copying – but 'something rather higher'.
Many famous pictures are not 'original' in the absolute sense – the artist may be
copying a set style, or have done a number of very similar studies. In this age of
high-tech copying, the distinction between a copy and an original is becoming
increasingly hypothetical.

In 'aesthetics' – the branch of philosophy concerned with defining beauty and art (the
word comes from a Greek one concerning 'perception') – the question is often
jargonised as whether beauty is objective, in which case we really ought to learn to
appreciate it, or subjective and emotional, in which case one person's view is as good
as anyone else's. It is between those who believe that 'beauty is out there', led by
Plato, who has Socrates explain in the *Phaedo*: 'it is by beauty that beautiful things are
beautiful', versus the 'dunnomuchabout (coff) butinowotilike' branch of relativism.
Indeed, if beauty is subjective, we have to accept the authority of general opinion.

One variation on the theme of the reality of beauty is the view that something that
functions well is more beautiful than something that either does not function
properly, or works but has unnecessary, inefficient bits. So, for example, a fit
healthy person is more beautiful than a pale, flabby one, and a rectangular

concrete bunker is more beautiful than an ornate medieval cathedral, with all its non-functional pinnacles, gargoyles and over-large windows. The early twentieth-century 'Bauhaus' art movement in Germany held something like this to be the case, and produced many interesting examples of functional, even 'brutalist' objects, such as uncomfy armchairs.

The ancient Greeks attached such importance to 'beauty' that they made the study of it compulsory for the ruling classes, and their legacy still ensures a role for 'art', 'drama' and 'music' in many schools today. But increasingly the contemporary activities of art, music and drama have moved on, to a point where they may no longer even intend to be about 'beauty'. Artists produce works out of disgusting objects designed to 'shock and challenge'; musicians produce sounds to provoke and accompany street violence and rape; whilst the most popular form of drama is the ceaseless round of arguments and petty cruelties that make for a good 'soap'. Since people like these ugly things, either they have become for them 'beautiful', or the people may have become, as Plato feared might happen, spiritually damaged and corrupted.

One particularly vexatious aesthetical issue is that of human beauty. Is it better to be blonde, buxom, fit and generally rather Aryan? Or petite, plump, dark and intelligent-looking? Built like a sumo-wrestler, or a sparrow? Golden brown, interestingly pale, or mysteriously dark? Pear, apple or banana shaped? Peach, aubergine or pomegranate skinned? Plato, wisely, had Socrates conclude that it's all a matter of each bit fitting with every other. It's not better in itself to be one thing or another, but it is better to find out what suits yourself.

An interesting perspective on all this was provided by the two Russian artists, Vitaly Komar and Alexander Melamid, who in 1996 challenged notions of 'high' and 'low' art by polling citizens of various countries on a range of artistic preferences and producing pictures to fit. So, for example, the one for the American market featured a (clothed) couple strolling leisurely through a soothing lakeside landscape, as a couple of deer frolic in the background.

Problem 32
Flash Bagman

This story – apart from its evidently rather slight interest in terms of 'copyright' and so on (a topic of pressing concern only to most people when they try to record music, or when their cheap 'counterfeit' jumper unravels or new 'Swiss' watch loses time) is an allegory. Allegory is one of those ancient Greek terms coming from two words meaning 'to address the other crowd'. An allegory is a story which has two meanings – a surface one and an underlying one. Because the surface story propels the listener along on its own terms, it is a useful way of conveying what may be difficult or controversial material in the 'hidden' allegory. One of the finest examples in literature of allegory is George Orwell's *Animal Farm*, where the animals revolt against their exploitative two-legged owner and decide to run the farm along socialist lines. Before long, however, the pigs take over the running of the farm, even moving into the farmhouse and eating at his table, and the other animals, such as poor Dobbin, the honest workhorse, find themselves working long hours under their tyrannical rule. It is all, of course, an allegory for the Russian Revolution.

Sometimes the relationship between the 'true' story and the allegorical one is exact, but more often it is metaphorical. In *Animal Farm*, the animals paint their ten founding principles on the barn door, and one by one the pigs (at night) rewrite them. No such document was ever written, but 'metaphorically' speaking the new rulers of Russia did redefine the founding values of the new society, for example, permitting the Communist Party caste to become 'superior' to the workers.

So what is the allegory in my little story? Ah, like the best such tales, that is for the reader to decide. But who is the 'prima donna', or person, like the actor in an opera, who thinks they should be the media star? It is surely Bagman. Dobbin after all up to then was content just to share his 'Curious Questions' with anyone who happened to come along at lunchtime.

Problems 33–34
The value of stamps and potatoes, I and II

The value of things is often artificially separated into a 'hard' economic or monetary value and a more shifting and unstable moral (or judgemental) value. Artificially, because economic values are concealed moral and aesthetic judgements. None the less, the illusion remains that the price, say of potatoes, is fairly fixed, whereas the price of a stamp may fluctuate because of the vagaries of fashion, and the value of something important like a chimpanzee, or even a human being, is complexly indeterminate!

Problems 35–40
Paradoxical picture puzzles

Whatever philosophers say, we know the real world is real. We can touch it, taste it or see it, for example. But even this reassuring common sense is actually a bit suspect, as these pictures help to show.

What we experience, psychologists say, is actually very different from what we get from our sense organs. We perceive a world of objects and events, separated in space and in time. But our senses actually take in an unsegregated flux. An example of this is speech. We hear words, and sentences, but their sound waves actually show that words and sentences are often joined seamlessly together, with any gaps there are appearing in the middle of words.

Ludwig Wittgenstein (in the *Philosophical Investigations*) used a rather inferior version of a duck, which, turned on its side, looks like a rabbit (sort of) to raise the issue of whether what one (duck-seeing) person sees is the *same* as that seen by a rabbit-seeing-person.

We create a stable world even though the sense information is constantly changing. Even as we walk round a room, objects are throwing themselves around and disappearing – but our brain corrects this to give the impression of stability. Part of this is an essential 'filling in the gaps' process that means we experience things that are not even there. A humdrum example of this is the 'triangle' of Problem 35. And conversely, we disregard things that are there, as shown in the figure/ground reversal of Problem 36. A slightly different sensory instance of this is the age-old philosophical problem of water that appears hot when 'in fact' it is very cold.

Actually, a similar trick known by psychologists is done with 'the Kaniszsa Square'. Even babies are able to recognise the 'square shape', and will gurgle excitedly when shown four circles (like 'Pacmen') with quarters cut out and arranged in the appropriate squarish way. This shows, the philosopher might add in measured tones, that the baby has the concept of *squareness*.

Problem 35
The cube and the triangle

The eye likes the second cube best. In fact, it's quite hard to see the first one as a cube, so dependent is visual perception on rules and clues. With the triangle, the clues are there but the object isn't necessarily.

Problem 36
Figure/ground reversal

Is it a Lady in White – or two of Zeno's Dancing Girls (in rather less), with feather boas?

This is an example of the well-known vase/profile type of picture, like that of the Danish psychologist Edgar Rubin, which alternately looks like two heads or a vase. Although it *is* a funny sort of vase.

Psychologists might say that what you see reflects the way your mind works, which, of course, it does. Sometimes the visual 'clues' are contradictory, and the interpretation can switch to and fro in a confusing way, displeasing to experience. The brain *does not like* pictures which can fluctuate from one to the other very much.

Problem 37
The false leg

The problem for Elvis is that he is tricked by the seam of his trousers into thinking he has another leg. Elvis is also holding two magical items, a wholly impossible triangle, and a slightly impossible magic wand.

This picture illustrates one of the highest forms of artistic representation – the cartoon. The highest, because the art of the cartoon is to convey a sense of reality with a minimum of effort and a maximum of implication. Powerful communication is by just a few lines, a few two-dimensional squiggles.

In this picture, the main visual trick is the 'third leg'. But equally false is the sense of Elvis being suspended (conveyed by just a few vertical lines at the top), and indeed the sense of movement and vitality of the whole figure itself.

The simplicity and purity of the cartoon is perhaps best exemplified by the celebrated Tintin books of Hergé, in which the stories of the boy reporter and his white dog are just the uppermost layer. These cartoons are now recognised as forms of art in their own right. But as art, Hergé in turn was drawing on the Chinese artists' notion of the 'clear line'. And of all 'clear lines', the clearest and most precise come from the papercut artist, whose little-understood but intricate creations must always respect the limitations of form imposed by their chosen medium.

Papercuts

Zheng Juchen, of the Chinese Academy of Fine Arts, tells the story of a traditional papercut artist, now in his eighties, living a simple but poor life in a run-down mud-walled hut, lined on the inside with old newspapers (as was the practical habit to stop the walls crumbling).

But this hut was distinguished from its many neighbours by two things. One was it retained the old wooden window where the others had adopted metal or plastic ones, a window of small panes still made of thin paper, not glass. And the old window suited the artist for it was the papercut itself that made up the panels, turning it into a superb stained glass window. An entire Peking Opera of aristocrats, warriors and cunning government officials which sprang to life as the sun shone through and turned the hut into a kaleidoscope of colour and movement.

And in the midst of it all, the old man cutting and singing to himself, completely self-sufficient and absorbed, acting out the characters even as the scissors freed their images. As Zheng put it in his book *Papercuts: The Art and Life*,* the old man

* Zhejiang People's Art Publishing House, 2002, published in Chinese only.

and his art were as one. For 'the creation of art needs inspiration, and inspiration is ecstatic madness'.

In general, however, as Zheng observes, it is very difficult for artists to get to this state of inspiration. Yet, somehow, this old papercutter was able to enter that crazy state simply by stepping into his parallel paper world. All he required was a sheet of paper and a pair of scissors in order to transcend the limitations and hardship of his reality.

Problem 38
The chair

Through the first peephole can be seen what appears to be a rudimentary chair. This the participants report. They are then asked to confirm their impression by looking through another three peepholes, all of which seem to show the rudimentary chair from slightly different angles, and their conviction becomes reinforced. But when they look through the fifth peephole – a shock is in store. The chair has disappeared, replaced by a meaningless collection of lines and shapes.

If it were not for the fact that, through the last peephole, the chair has reappeared, this time seen from above, they might imagine the chair has simply been blown up by the experimenters, but clearly, all the views are of the same thing, and can be repeated.

All the time, the chair is a figment of their imaginations. Actually, all there is through the peepholes are suspended strings and shapes painted on walls. The chair is such a plausible image that their brains quickly create one out of the limited evidence presented to their eyes. Psychologists like to say that 'perception is largely an hypothesis-making process'.

Actually, the idea of peepholes occurred to Mary Midgley, a contemporary philosopher noted for disparaging the omnipotence of scientists. She once wrote that human life was like watching fish in a big aquarium. Her idea was that looking through the little windows that are set into these giant fish tanks (with dolphins and sharks often to be glimpsed swimming around in them) is similar to using different ways of thinking – scientific, historic, philosophic – to try to interpret the world. 'Fish and other strange creatures constantly swim away from particular windows . . . reappearing where different lighting may make them hard to recognize', she says with evident echoes of Plato's famous metaphor of the prisoners in the cave who bemusedly watch flickering shadows thrown on the wall.

Midgley herself assumes that each of the peepholes or perspectives lends some additional insight, and that the important thing is to use them all, for 'if we refuse to put together the data from different windows, then we can be in real trouble', she explains. But as our phantom chair experiment shows, reality may be more complicated than that.

Note on the Philosophical Pictures

In this edition, a new picture introducing each section has been added. Drawn especially to illustrate the philosophical texts by the French artist, Judit, each one provides proof that there are verily two parts to the brain, if not the mind, one to process images, one to process words, and the one that processes images is much more powerful. I like to think that, in this way, we add both a new dimension and a new way of approaching the problems.

Problem 39
Band with a twist in it

It appears to have only one surface now. However, if you cut the band in two along the middle you can now colour one side green and the other side black. And it is twice as big!* The strip is sometimes known as the 'Möbius strip' and can be used to illustrate – for example by drawing a left and right hand on the strip and trying to superimpose them on each other – how left- and right-handedness, that most basic feature of the universe, is a topological feature – i.e. you can get around it by cutting the strip.

---

* Actually, when I tried this, it didn't work. Although twice as big a loop, instead of getting rid of the twist, as hoped, it added another. The reader may like to consult an expert, instead (a junior school teacher, perhaps?).

Problem 40
'The blobs' and 'The colour disk illusion'

Sometimes known as *the grid illusion* – nasty grey splodges appear before the eyes! This is due to what is sometimes termed the 'excitation of the rods and cones' in the eyes. What we see depends on what's next to it.

Make a copy of the disk, cut it out, stick onto a piece of card and make a hole in the middle.* Stick a sharpened pencil through this and if you spin the disk you should see some remarkably bright colours. The colours we see depend on motion, too. Psychologists have found that if people are put in a room papered with different shades of grey, lit with a red lightbulb, they see the walls not only as grey, but red and green as well (which could save on paint).

These last problems, despite their resemblance to children's tricks, could still, arguably, be said to give more of an insight into our flawed notions of 'reality' than the complete works of Kant, Hegel and Heidegger rolled into one, cut along the centre, with a pencil stuck through the middle of it.

But for philosophers there are (at least) two fairly tricky problems about colour. One is whether it really is 'out there', or is only 'in here'? In the mind of the beholder, or made up of little electromagnetic vibrations? Anyway, what difference is there between a real sensation of colour and an imaginary one? (Are the grey blobs or the colours on the colour disk real or imaginary?) Not to forget colour-blind people who see green as red, and animals, who hardly see colours at all. Worse still, what's true of colours is also true for all the other sense perceptions, even if John Locke *et al.* have tried to mark colour off as a special case of unreliable knowledge.

Problems 41–44
Time

Time travel is a fascinating subject. (See also 'Time' in the Glossary as well as the

---

* Actually, 'customer feedback' has revealed that the earlier (editions 1 and 2) versions of the disk simply did not work! Hence, the third edition has been re-drawn more scientifically, to recreate the flickeing of black and white that creates colours in our minds.

'Elementary Problems of Natural Philosophy' later.) Quite sensible sub-atomic physicists discuss it all the 'time', which is where the term 'worm-holes' comes from. (A worm-hole is a natural 'time machine' – a gap in the space-time continuum just big enough for a sub-atomic particle to slip through.) There are even some physicists who have measured particles going faster than the speed of light, at which rate, general relativity tells us, they should start to go back in time. But then, really, we all travel through time anyway.

Problem 42
The time-stopper

Clearly, as Lucy realises, what is needed is to travel slower than everyone else for a while, so that when we have gone, say, a day, the rest of the world has gone a thousand years. That would then provide a novel perspective, at least. As Dr Wenn is perhaps thinking, this is fairly straightforward, involving little more than cryogenics. At the moment, science allows us to freeze embryos for as long as we like, effectively putting a person into suspended animation – the dream of the 'sleepers' who are supposedly deep-frozen in various vaults in California may not be so far off the mark. (Although that won't help them.) But it does not really seem to be time travel. Certainly, in the absence of a way of travelling back, it is not much use.

Problem 43
The microworld time forgot

Dr Wenn's explanation of why he cannot invent a machine to travel back in time is novel, but he then undermines it by appearing to have achieved it, albeit only in his 'microworld'. Probably his point is that time, like space, is relative, so that although it is only possible to go forward in time, it is possible to appear to be going backwards relative to something else. Just as sometimes when you are on a train in a station and another train next to you moves off, you imagine for a moment that your train is actually going backwards. The only way you can tell 'the difference' is if you look at the station buildings. Perhaps, Dr Wenn's point is, with time, there are no 'station buildings' or fixed points.

This may seem a very odd idea, but then think of watching a TV show. It is broadcast this year, on 1 January. But if your TV set is on a spaceship circling the nearest star,

Discussions

it will not be 'broadcast' until four years from now. Similarly, when you look up at the night sky, the stars you see may have ceased to exist several thousand years ago – the light you see is thousands of years old.

Theoretical physicists, who are today's 'philosophers of nature' (see Problems 91–95) have their own, even more weedy, 'microworlds' in which they say time flows backwards. In their atomic colliders, sub-atomic particles split into other particles and recombine a bit later, producing or absorbing energy. For example, a particle of light or a photon, moving forward in time, spontaneously splits into a positron and an electron. The electron carries on its own way, whilst the positron encounters another electron and combines in a puff of light energy into a new photon. For mathematicians anyway, there is no difference between this and simply allowing the 'arrow of time' to be reversed, so that we can now quite happily describe exactly the same events as an electron going back in time. (If you don't understand all these different particles, do not be too alarmed. Physicists simply invent them to fill the gaps in their equations and their existence is a moot point.)

Problem 44
The unreliable watches

The problem, the physicists say, is that Mr Megasoft upset the space-time continuum by flying around. He is not entitled to a refund.

Since the discovery in the nineteenth century (see Problem 91) that light always travels at a constant speed, and Einstein's incorporation of this fact into his General Theory of Relativity, it has been accepted that time flows at different rates depending on gravity, and also is affected by that special form of gravity caused by constant acceleration. (Time is even thought to actually 'stop' in the centre of a 'black hole', those bits of the universe where gravity is so intense that not even light can escape its clutches.) By flying around, Mr Megasoft has experienced both types of variation in the space-time continuum, and it is hardly surprising that his watch has recorded the fact.

The first atomic clocks using caesium were made in the 1950s and these days they have many practical applications, particularly in navigation, just as it was with earlier chronographs. However, it was not until 1971 that two scientists, J. C. Hafele and Richard Keating, tried flying them right the way around the world in a passenger jet, sometimes eastbound and sometimes westbound, and found that the clock in the westbound flight gained not just one but an appalling 273 nano-seconds (that is, billionths of a second), as certain a result as anything in physics can be – baffling though its consequences are. For example, if one twin went off on a spaceship, perhaps Mr Megasoft's space yacht, to a suitable star and came back, say, fifty years later having experienced sustained high acceleration, this twin would find that they were physically no longer like the twin left at home – they would be many years younger! (This is sometimes known as 'The twins paradox'.) For philosophers, the everyday sense of 'absolute time' is reduced to little more than an earthbound prejudice.

In this example, and in the Hafele and Keating experiment, the major factors are the altitude and the reduced gravitational pull rather than the acceleration of the plane, which is negligible most of the time. Because of the earth's rotation, it also makes a difference which compass direction you travel in.

Problem 45
The mind's eye

Actually, I can't remember lots of other things I have done. John Locke's contemporary, Thomas Reid, pointed out very quickly that he sometimes forgot what he was doing, but did that make him a different person? Surely not, it would be absurd. And then there's another 'bonus' problem attached by saying that people are bound together by their memories of themselves and what they have done. Sometimes their memory is wrong. A wannabe surfer may 'remember' themselves looking tanned and magnificent riding the biggest wave of the summer in to the beach in a triumphant finish – even though in fact (after a large lunch and several ice-cream sundaes) they barely managed to stand up for a few seconds as a small breaker trundled in past the headland.

Perhaps it would be better to say, as David Hume put it, 'memory does not so much "produce" as "discover" personal identity'. The trouble with that is that it leaves the real question unanswered.

Which may not look much of a philosophy problem, but, in fact, has been extensively considered by many philosophers over the centuries, and has been given not one but three names, which is rather a 'problem of identity' in itself. Sometimes it is called the 'problem of personal identity', sometimes 'the problem of the self' and oft-times indeed 'the problem of self-knowledge'.

Problem 46
A more corporeal problem

Clearly, that would not do.

A serious philosopher adds:

Why is this discussion so short? It is surely worth mentioning some of Derek Parfit's views, and maybe Bernard Williams' response? Didn't Strawson define 'identity' in his book Individuals *(1959) as 'the concept of a type of entity such that both predicates ascribing states of consciousness and predicates ascribing corporeal characteristics, a physical situation, etc. are equally applicable to a single individual of that single type'?*

But we can do better than that, and return to David Hume, for his answer to the various questions of 'personal identity': 'Where am I, or when? From what causes do I devise my existence, and to what condition shall I return?'

> I am confounded with all these questions, and begin to fancy myself in the most deplorable condition imaginable, environ'ed with the deepest darkness, and utterly depriv'd of the use of every member and faculty.
> Most fortunately it happens, that since reason is incapable of dispelling these clouds, nature herself suffices to that purpose, and cures me of this philosophical melancholy and delirium, either by relaxing this bent of mind, or by some avocation, and lively impression of the senses, which obliterate all these chimeras.

And how!

> I dine, I play a game of back-gammon, I converse and am merry with my friends; and when after three or four hours amusement, I would return to these speculations, they appear so cold and strained, and ridiculous, that I cannot find in my heart to enter into them any further.

Problems 47–48
The book, I and II

Since Gibb's book has initially been rejected irrespective of the intentions of the author, the evidence that has now accumulated in favour of the book is not necessarily conclusive. Probably the schools still won't touch it. Some could say it has become too 'political'. And in others, educational experts might point out that children may not understand it and still pick up racist attitudes. In writing, the intentions of the author, whatever Emerald may think, don't really count for much. The book has a life of its own.

But that is still to suppose that it is someone's job to protect children from certain points of view or undesirable influences. Marlborough library in Wiltshire found – after complaints by parents – that a book had crept into its young children's section featuring baby-battering and the murder of a policeman. The *Punch and Judy* book was removed from the shelves.

Plato was notoriously one of the first to advocate constructive social censorship, not just for children but for the whole of his idealised 'republic'. And indeed censorship is alive and well all over the world. Computers and the internet in particular are also introducing all sorts of problems of privacy and control. As the long-anticipated Information Society becomes a reality, policy makers and legislators have been struggling to retain control.

Internet users in China have been obliged to send their communications through special ports and filters that are under the government's watchful eye. Similar systems of filtration have been developed by Vietnam, Iran, Saudi Arabia and several of the other Gulf states. The French government is trying to curb the use of English in its 'national cyberspace', whilst in the United States, Germany and Japan, legislators are constantly fighting against 'indecent' material. In the UK children are protected from a wide range of 'unsuitable' material, including unsolicited electronic mail. But, interestingly, few countries agree on just what it is that their citizens need to be protected from.

Perhaps what the story of *Little Black Sheep* shows is that censorship is a two-way process. It is not so much the book or the programme that needs to be controlled – it is the reaction of the reader or viewer. And, of course, that varies unpredictably from person to person.

Problem 49
Sleeping problems

Philosophers have always been very interested in what people are able to do when they are asleep. This is less because most people spend more time asleep than listening to philosophical arguments, and some, indeed, combine both functions, but more because, in sleep, the soul is freed, as it were, from the chains of earthly sense experience, free to attain philosophical truths. As Kant put it in the *Critique of Practical Reason*, in 'deepest sleep, perhaps the greatest perfection of the mind might be exercised in rational thought'. On the other hand, as St Thomas noted, 'if a man syllogises while asleep, when he wakes up he invariably recognises a flaw in some respect', and, as Socrates asked Glaucon, 'Does not dreaming consist in mistaking the semblance of reality for reality itself?'

In the *Philosophical Investigations*, Wittgenstein too thought that knowledge obtained in dreams was unreliable because it might not be accurately remembered. So what can people do whilst they are asleep? Can they answer simple questions?

Aristotle believed that someone who was asleep could both distinguish between a man and a horse, ugly or beautiful, white or not white (*Metaphysics*, 485b). Descartes wrote, in the *Discourse on Method*, that 'all the same thoughts and conceptions which we have while awake may also come to us in sleep', as well as, in a letter: 'I had good reason to assert that the human soul is always conscious in any circumstances, even in the mother's womb'. More recently, Freud diagnosed in *A General Introduction to Psychoanalysis* (1943) that 'Dreams are the mode of reaction of the mind to stimuli acting upon it during sleep'.

But Descartes ultimately decided in the *Meditations*, that since God was 'supremely good and cannot err', i.e. not nasty, the false information obtained in the dreamylands must still be possible for a rational person to distinguish from the (supposedly) tidy, coherent knowledge of the world we live in. This confidence neither Leibniz nor Bertrand Russell shared, Leibniz saying that 'it is not impossible, metaphysically speaking, that there may be a dream as continuous and as lasting as the life of a man'. Or indeed, as the life of a butterfly. The greatest exponent of butterfly dreams being the ancient Chinese sage, Chang Tzu (see the discussion of Problem 13).

One of Wittgenstein's (few) friends, Norman Malcolm, in his study of *Dreaming* (Routledge, 1959) thought maybe saying 'I am asleep' is like saying 'I am dead', meaningless self-contradictory nonsense. The passenger on the train who says 'I am awake' is suspect: for the opposite claim, 'I am asleep', by being meaningless, leaves it without 'its proper negation'. 'Certainly', Norman Malcolm continues, 'you cannot be said to know by observation that you are awake because if you could it would make sense to speak of knowing by observation that you are not awake'.

Problems 50–51
Still indisposed

This may not seem like much of a problem to us, if we are just interested in what people actually do. And to get the police involved may seem like an overreaction. But if, for example, a judge is asked to consider whether Steve is basically a decent sort who has been led astray by his assertiveness training, exacerbated by side effects from taking drugs, then we may be obliged to move away from the notion that people have 'free will'. Jean-Paul Sartre, the French author-philosopher, produced some monumental defences of free will, all couched in bizarre, occasionally beautiful but more often incomprehensible 'existentialist' language. His view was that we are all free to do what we like, but choose or allow ourselves, like an overzealous waiter in a cafe, to follow roles.

Increasingly, instead of this view of human nature, really a legal fiction, where people make choices and are held responsible for them, Western societies move towards one where people's behaviour is largely determined by other outside factors, for which they cannot be held entirely responsible.

The judge may be confronted by extremely plausible scientific evidence that Steve is suffering from one of the 300 mental syndromes, now on offer in the *Diagnostic and Statistical Manual of Mental Disorders*, the 'bible' of American psychiatry. This slim volume of just over a hundred disorders in the mid-1970s, has grown rather fat with the discovery of numerous new 'paranoid personality disorders'. These range from 'Asperger's syndrome' which is a kind of acute shyness, to very unshy behaviour such as something called 'frotteurism' – a desire to rub oneself in a sexual manner against fellow passengers on public transport! One of the most serious disorders is compulsive shopping syndrome, which 'the bible' says is a genetically determined compulsion, affecting an astonishing one in twelve Americans. Like gambling addiction or even pyromania (love of fire), it is said to be 'caused' by chemicals like serotonin being released in the brain. And the symptoms? Large debts at the bank and a pile of things in the cupboard (typically fashion items and electrical equipment) you can't even remember buying, let alone why. (Of course the debts could *also* have something to do with paying the psychiatrist's bill, but perhaps we'd do better to suppress these thoughts in the subconscious mind.)

Or it could be that Steve has developed a phobia, one of the growing number of scientifically recognised causes of 'panic attacks'. In the footsteps of agoraphobia and claustrophobia, even arachnophobia (the fears respectively, of being in the open or in enclosed spaces, or of spiders), comes anthophobia, which most of my neighbours seem to have ('fear of plants'), ecclesio and hiero phobias, which seem to be on the increase (churches or priests), ombrophobia, which is a good reason not to live in England (rain), and even pogonphobia, which raises ethical issues (fear of beards).

Nevertheless, the judge will still need to decide whether Steve was acting as himself – or not – that day.

Problem 52
The sleeping man

The philosopher John Locke (1632–1704) used a rather more modest example of a sleeping man to illustrate the complexities of the question of whether we are ever truly free to make our choices, or whether actually behaviour is 'determined' by factors such as genetics, social pressure or straightforward physical forces. A good example of this is a teacher who decides to teach children the importance of reading the words of a revolutionary leader. They may do this because they think the leader's words are important – or simply because, if they don't, they will risk getting the sack. It is hard to know which!

Isaiah Berlin (1909–97) discusses it in his convoluted essay, 'Two Concepts of Liberty', where he compares 'negative freedom' – no actual constraints (the door is not actually locked) – which is the concern of liberals, such as John Stuart Mill in *On Liberty*, with 'positive freedom', the old Stoic concept of managing not to want something anyway, which is what the sleeping man achieves here. (Berlin is against both of them.)

Problem 53
A problem arranging ship battles

At first sight, the philosopher's best line is that Cassandra's claims are indeed true – or false – but that no one, on earth at least, can know which so they may as well suit themselves. But clearly the gullible people have decided that she is the better judge of which it is, so this option is shut off.

The problem is, *if* the warnings are 'true' when Cassandra makes them, the events have then *got* to happen, and there is nothing anyone can do about it. 'And that is a problem for that philosophically tricky concept of "free will", which is why this counts as a personal problem'.

Aristotle originally discussed all this in 'Of Interpretations', *De Interpretatione*, part IX 186, where he briefly mentions the example of a ship battle.

Problems 54 and 55
Deep Thought speaks for itself and Deeper thought

So can computers think anyway? A lot of people think they can, in fact there is a whole branch of philosophy (or more accurately, off philosophy) called 'cognitive science' largely devoted to the study of 'artificial intelligence'.

The only thing special, it seems, about humans is that they are 'conscious', although quite what difference that makes is anyone's guess. Probably, the difference is less important than supposing that there is one. This allows us to treat computers as inanimate objects, devoid of rights.

In the sixteenth century, Michel de Montaigne (1533–92) wrote that from 'similar effects we should conclude that there are similar faculties'. Consequently, 'we should admit that animals employ the same method and the same reasoning as ourselves when we do anything'.

Animals, of course, are also not allowed normal rights, even though they move around, they appear to have preferences (make value-judgements) and exhibit all the symptoms of suffering. We know a lot about this because psychologists and other scientists have very carefully measured the effects of maltreating animals.

The former sometimes use apparatus like the Skinner Box, a cage with an electrified floor in which dogs are subjected to electric shocks if they press the wrong button – or, indeed, the right button depending on the experiment (one favourite is to train animals one way, and then change the rules, to see what happens!)

Animal rights is a divisive issue, with the consensus of opinion around the biblical view of animals being there for our use, in any way we like. Kant placed animals outside the 'moral community', but still warned against cruelty on the grounds of 'self-corruption'. The alternative position of all animals having similar rights to human beings, which is also taken by some religions, has certain practical problems associated with it, not least that in refusing to recognise a distinction between humans and everything else, it must also rule out distinctions between, say, mosquitoes and rabbits.

Even the entirely practical and limited position of minimising animal suffering is not always accepted, on the grounds that animals do not really suffer because they lack self-consciousness. If you put, say, a dog in front of a mirror, it will not learn that it is its own reflection it can see. The fox being chased by the hounds is said not to suffer, but to exhibit merely mechanical distress. (Peter Singer, the 'animal rights' philosopher, has described the apparent hypocrisy of theories of justice which leave animals out in the cold.) Deep Thought does not need to produce plaintive whines for us to know that it is conscious, though. Indeed, it would be easy enough to make even the most humble computer speak self-referentially on being switched on: 'I am conscious now – I await instructions.' Indeed, we can imagine a computer having little difficulty recognising its reflection given the necessary mechanical appendages.

The American philosopher, John Searle, discussed what has become known as the Chinese Room test for judging where computers deserved to be considered intelligent, following on from a discussion initiated by the Second World War code-breaker and philosopher, Alan Turing. Searle described the possibilities of communicating with an Anglo-someone in another room using written Chinese – the idea being that this illustrates what it is like to be a computer. The person in the room doesn't understand Chinese, but has a list of rules relating to recognising the symbol that is posted in to the room and then, using their rule book, posts back the appropriate Chinese response. To the person outside the room, the one inside appears to be understanding their questions although, in fact, they are merely behaving like machines – or dogs. Turing suggests that when we are unable to tell the difference after prolonged questioning of whether we are talking to a machine or to a human being, we ought to consider the computer to have intelligence. Searle's argument is that the person in the room does not understand Chinese. This is fairly convincing as, after all, at the beginning of his example, he states that they 'know no Chinese, either written or spoken', and that for them, 'Chinese writing is just so many meaningless squiggles'. This may seem a bit like stating the obvious, but then analytic philosophers do that sort of stuff. The trick is to make the obvious seem not so obvious.

But what seems to have been missed is not that the person in the room appears to understand Chinese, but that the whole 'system' – person in the room, sets of symbols on cards, plus instructions taped to the wall – gives the appearance of understanding it. And this is much more plausible. After all, the person who wrote the instructions did understand Chinese. What may have happened is that the expertise of the Chinese speaker has been transferred.

This makes it much more difficult for Searle, or anyone else, to deny the computer any expertise or even 'understanding'. (And actually, these days, you may be treated in hospitals, given career advice, told where to dig for gold or whatever, by a computer using 'expert systems' of rules and procedures drawn from human expertise.)

And, anyway, computers have been able to bamboozle people convincingly for a long time. In the 1960s, Joseph Weizenbaum, an American artificial intelligence researcher, developed a number of programs mimicking psychotherapy using a computer hardly more powerful than that controlling a toaster today. The programs accepted natural language from the user who typed on a typewriter, and responded with what appeared to be natural language via a printer. The most celebrated of these programs was Eliza, a program that was modelled on psychotherapy. Eliza generally returned whatever people typed in in a slightly different order, perhaps having picked out a keyword. The purely random responses of 'Yeses' and 'Noes' was interpreted as deep thought. Simple though the program was, it became very popular. Psychiatrists adopted it as the basis for actual therapy sessions. Users became attached to and dependent on Eliza, and computer pundits cited it as an example of how computers could learn to 'talk'. This is one of the actual 'conversations' (quoted from *Computer Power and Human Reason*, by Joseph Weizenbaum, published by W. Freeman, San Francisco, 1976):

156

PATIENT: Men are all alike.

ELIZA [Computer]:   *In what way?*

PATIENT: They're always bugging us about something or other.

ELIZA: *Can you think of a specific example?*

PATIENT: Well, my boyfriend made me come here.

ELIZA: *Your boyfriend made you come here?*

PATIENT: He says I'm depressed all the time.

ELIZA: *I am sorry to hear you are depressed.*

PATIENT: It's true I am unhappy.

ELIZA: *Do you think coming here will help you not to be unhappy?*

PATIENT: I need some help, that much seems certain.

ELIZA: *What would it mean to you if you got some help?*

PATIENT: Perhaps I could learn to get along with my mother.

ELIZA: *Tell me more about your family.*

PATIENT: My mother takes care of me.

ELIZA: *Who else in your family takes care of you?*

PATIENT: My father.

ELIZA: *Your father?*

PATIENT: You are like my father in some way.

ELIZA: *What resemblance do you see?*

PATIENT: You are not very aggressive but I don't think you want me to notice that.

ELIZA: *What makes you think I am not very aggressive?*

PATIENT: You don't argue with me.

ELIZA: *Why do you think I don't argue with you?*

PATIENT: You are afraid of me.

ELIZA: *Does it please you to believe I am afraid of you?*

PATIENT: My father is afraid of everybody.

ELIZA: *What else comes to mind when you think of your father?*

PATIENT: Bullies.

ELIZA: *Does that have anything to do with the fact that your boyfriend made you come here?*

After this experience, Weizenbaum decided that computers should not be allowed to give responses that appear 'human'. 'What I had not realised is that extremely short exposure to a relatively simple computer program could induce powerful delusional thinking in quite normal people.'

The secret of Weizenbaum's programs was that it is quite easy to appear intelligent, simply by repeating what the person talking to you has just said, but making it look like something different. Naturally, psychotherapists would dispute the power of the computer to communicate meaningfully, but for the rest of us it seems to show that the Searle test was passed before it was even devised.

The criterion for allowing computers rights will need to be something different. Possibly something that allows a few of the animals back into the fold of sentient beings. In the meantime, it looks as if the computer will have to be allowed its money.

Problems 56–59
Paradoxical pictures

The Dutch artist M. C. Escher (1898–1972) is famous for his paradoxical pictures. Despite their mathematical sophistication and value, Escher's mind was too free-roaming to follow any system, and he himself was hopeless at maths. Anyway, Escher believed the human mind was at its best when playing or being joking and self-mocking. He hoped that in doing this his pictures might have in them an element of truth. His pictures present empirical reality as illusory in many respects but, at the same time, there is a suggestion of an underlying structure and order to the universe.

Problem 56
Daytime – or night-time?

In this one, he explores the effects of reversals. Escher uses a series of interlocking diamond shapes which gradually evolve to become a series of black or white birds. These are each other's mirror image as well, and are flying off in opposite directions.

As the birds approach the sides of the picture, they release themselves from the flock and swoop down to become part of the landscape beneath, the white ones part of the day, the black ones part of the night. At the same time, the landscape begins to produce new birds, the second aspect of an intermeshed perpetual cycle.

Professor Frank Close, a nuclear physicist investigating the origins of the universe by banging particles together, thinks this image is also a good model for one of the fundamental questions of modern science. If, he points out, you took a negative copy of the picture, so that black became white and white black, you would obtain a mirror image of what you started with. Indeed, look at the negative image in a mirror, and you see the original picture again. Now, if the white geese are thought of as matter, and the black geese as anti-matter, and the process of copying is the first zillionth of a second in the history of the universe, what seems to have happened is that the geese mutated slightly, leaving a little more matter than anti-matter behind. And that matter is the universe. Escher's picture illustrates symmetry, and symmetry, the atomic physicists think, is the key to understanding the universe – which is also what the ancient philosophers of India, China and Greece were working on.

Problem 57
But will the waterfall?

Unfortunately not. In *Waterfall*, Escher links three 'impossible triangles' to create the illusion that the water is continually flowing away from the viewer. The catch is that each corner of the impossible triangle is 90°. Escher uses perspective to skew the image to make it *look* possible when, in the normal world, it isn't. *Waterfall* also illustrates the feature of many paradoxes, that taken bit by bit, there is nothing apparently objectionable. It is only taken as a whole that we, as Escher put it, 'discover any mistake in it'.

Problem 58
The architect's secret

Also by Escher. The ladder is inside at the ground floor, but outside at the top, and the columns aren't much better either . . . Escher himself wanted to be an architect, but failed his exams. If he had passed them his creations would (probably) have been less interesting.

Problem 59
The three hares illusion

The three hares illustrate again how the eye creates images in the mind. Here, the image is totally satisfying, yet *logically* we know something is wrong.

Curiously, the 'three rabbits' (or three hares) has been around for thousands of years as a design, often in churches. On seeing our excellent version, constructed by Molehill in their factories in Brighton, David Singmaster, a professor of mathematics no less, told me of some he has found, starting with a Sui Dynasty (AD 581–618) ceiling painting of the three rabbits in which the whole group seems to be whirling.

Another fine one, 600 years later, in the north of England, in the ancient cathedral town of Lincoln, is a design of three lizards (or maybe little dragons), each eating the body of the next one.

To explain the design's appearance in churches, some people say it symbolises the Christian Trinity. But for others it represents the trivium, which is an old term for studying the three philosophical arts of grammar, rhetoric and logic, from which I presume we get the word 'trivia', which literally means 'the place where three roads meet', and nowadays has the sense of 'collection of useless information'. So the three rabbits have become trivia, which is why there is a pub on Dartmoor which has the three rabbits design on its sign hanging outside the door, and sells T-shirts of it too. The attached note explains the design as chosen for the inn as it is near a rabbit warren, which says something about how ancient mysteries become banalised.

Mind you, I originally put it in the book simply because I liked it. (But then, why did I like it?)

Problems 36 and 59 also illustrate aspects of what is sometimes known as *perceptual stereotyping*. This is the process where the mind puts together incomplete data to arrive at a conclusion, a process which is essential but, at the same time, unreliable. And once a stereotype is identified, evidence which does not fit in with the idea is lost. A similar thing happens with other senses. Sound waves, for instance, reach us as undifferentiated babble, via those vibrations of the little bones in the inner ear. But it still takes a mental process to start to sort out the information, 'the signal', from the 'noise', which is also why hearing aids aren't as much help as they might be otherwise.

Perceptual stereotyping has much wider implications than being just visual trickery – if we think something is a log we may fail to notice it watching us, and be unpleasantly surprised when it opens a large mouth and bites our leg. On the other hand, creativity and originality rely on the same sort of illogical thinking.

Of the 'Twelve traditional philosophy problems no one really cares about anyway', Problems 60 and 61 raise issues over the 'properties' of things that don't exist in the usual sense. (They might also be of interest to literary types.) If something doesn't actually exist, can it have any characteristics? (Does sugar *really* grow on the hedges in Sugar Candy Land?) Some have argued that to say, for example, unicorns have one horn is really to say that if unicorns existed, they would have one horn. If the (present) King of France existed, then he would be bald.

If you're really interested . . .

Unicorns' horns

The nineteenth-century psychologist Alexis von Meinong (1853–1920) distinguished between two types of thing – those which have existed or do exist, like apples or himself, and those which don't, like unicorns or the present King of France – or, even more importantly, Sugar Candy Land. (Leaving aside the question of things which may exist in the future – see Problem 53.) This he further complicated by distinguishing between types of relationship, such as the relation (predictably) of the colours red and green. This, Meinong decided, is 'real' enough, but still does not 'exist'. Numbers too, are real, without existing. Then there is the question of 'factuality', such that whenever someone says something factual, we can say their statement is 'true'. Before we can decide the status of unicorns, we must decide which of these types of truth we are dealing with.

Naturally, none of this moves the debate on very far – but it does introduce some new terms for philosophers to juggle with. Meinong does some juggling himself, finishing with the flourish that truth is a purely human construct, but facts are eternal.

The King of France's pate

For some philosophers (notably, as well as von Meinong, one Edmund G. Husserl, 1859–1938) the King of France lies outside 'the realm of being', and normal rules do not apply to him. In particular, he can both be bald and not bald – at the same time! Bertrand Russell, as so often seems to have been his role, was appalled at this, and straight away set to working out a logical system for dealing with non-existent kings, unicorns *et al.* His resulting 'theory of descriptions' suggested that what was being 'denoted' in sentences like these was not the usual sort of thing at all, a grammatical 'subject', such as 'Louis XIV', or 'hippopotami', for example, but merely a claim about logical relationships. Something along the lines of:

> If there is a King of France, then he is bald
> *There is a King of France*
> Therefore, the King of France is bald

Russell puts it differently, preferring to put everything into the 'predicate':

> At least one thing is the King of France
> At most there is one thing that is the King of France
> Anything which is the King of France is bald OR
> There is nothing which is the King of France and not bald!

Other versions have it that 'there is exactly one person now reigning over France AND there is no one now reigning over France who is not bald' – we could go on indefinitely. None of which, fairly obviously, gets us anywhere so we leave it there, as Russell himself was obliged to do after rather more agonising.

Problem 62
Snow's colour

Clearly not, as any Inuit could say, but don't ask a philosopher. One who had a particularly strong view to the contrary, though, was Thomas Reid (1710–90). Reid held that snow really was white, saying (*Inquiry*, chapter 6, section 5) that the sensation of 'whiteness' is 'directly experienced as a mental process, an act which corresponds to the external object, rather than just being a mental intermediary between us and reality'.

These problems are all broadly concerned with 'truth'. As indeed are many of the other problems, such as 'The raven', 'The ship battle', 'The cow in the field' and so on. Being traditional in style, they do not really help to highlight the issues, but in passing we might recall Karl Popper's useful contribution to the debate around the time those most extreme philosophers of logic, the Logical Positivists, were holding court in Vienna, that if you cannot imagine showing that something is not the case, then it probably doesn't mean much to say that it is.

As Karl Popper puts it, in the *Poverty of Historicism*, taking issue with Descartes who thought it was enough to be very pleased with your theory (to see it 'clearly and distinctly'):

> tests can be interpreted as attempts to weed out false theories – to find the weak points of a theory in order to reject it if it is falsified by the test. This view is sometimes considered paradoxical; our aim, it is said, is to establish theories, not to eliminate false ones. But just because it is our aim to establish theories as well as we can, we must test them as severely as we can; that is, we must try to find fault with them. Only if we cannot falsify them despite our best efforts can we say they have stood up to severer tests. This is why a theory means very little if we have not tried, and failed, to discover refutations. For if we are uncritical, we shall always find what we want: we shall look for, and find confirmations, and we shall look away from and not see, whatever might be dangerous to our pet theories.
>
> (pp. 133–34, 1957, in 2nd edn, Routledge, 1960)

A good example of this kind of 'wishful theorising' is that surrounding the contemporary debate over the so-called 'greenhouse effect'. Scientists almost every week produce evidence apparently confirming the rapidity of global warming – unusual temperature in one place, melting glaciers in another, even the 'thinning of the ice caps' – and resolutely disregard as irrelevant data, such as exceptionally low temperatures in some areas, or the polar surveys showing ice cover remains normal – which is running against the theory. But be warned! Philosophers risk losing their halo of authority when they talk of such highly politicised 'scientific' issues.

Problem 63
Unmarried bachelors

Don't you believe it!

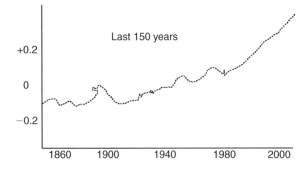

In which an alarming rise in temperature is confirmed . . .

Figure 2   Global temperatures

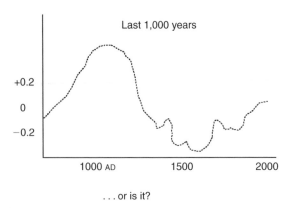

. . . or is it?

Problem 64
The author of *Waverley*

Er . . . but look in most Oxbridge inter-war philosophy books and you should be able to find out.

Problem 65
Martian water

Sometimes the funny water is not on Mars but on 'Twin-Earth' with its own kind of water with a different chemical composition.

Any book on philosophy problems – worth its salt – should include at least one version of the US professor Hilary Putnam's much discussed 'thought experiment'. Putnam it was who first envisaged another planet just like ours except for one thing – the water in it has the chemical formula XYZ!

Well . . .

Anyway, is it water or not?

There have been a lot of papers on this, evidently a very stimulating question, at least as far as most philosophical musings go. One goes on to say (sounding a bit like an advertising hoarding) that 'Hilary Putnam's "Twin-Earth" thought experiment is indispensable'. The author goes on to add that 'for some reason I don't know, virtually no one has responded to [the] argument that anti-supervenience rules out token identity physicalism'. He recalls that Davidson too (just surnames here) has quite a bit to say about Twin-Earth, believing that we can have, 'mental tokens as well as physical tokens with anti-supervenience', and mental tokens can have their non-supervenience necessarily. Our author regards this argument as a bit of a failure, and we can surely agree with that (although perhaps not for the same reasons).

Problem 66
The millennium problem

Possibly there is a confusion in the question here. The issue of whether something which is green up to teatime and blue afterwards can be described properly, has perplexed many philosophers, worried about the implications for experimental method and so on. David Hume, the eighteenth-century philosopher, wondered why we assume green things will still be green tomorrow, rather than fluctuating in colour. He pointed out that the arguments we use tend to assume that the future will resemble the past.

Problem 67
Green and red

This is a version of the great 'green/red all over' dilemma that has perplexed so many philosophers to so little effect. As far as the jumper goes, I actually *had* one that was green and red all over at the same time – it was striped. And there are other, even stronger, examples! Mathematicians believe two contradictory examples seem to do just this. They believe that a negative number multiplied by another negative number will make a positive number. In fact, they even think it's true by definition. Then, at the same time, they allow for negative numbers to have square roots, which essentially means to allow another negative number to be multiplied by itself and still remain negative. The square root of minus one is defined as being 'i' (rather than minus one again) – standing for imaginary number. They then use these imaginary numbers in a great many not at all imaginary situations.

Einstein once wrote (in a paper entitled 'Geometry and Experience'): 'as far as the propositions of mathematics refer to reality, they are not certain; and as far as they are certain, they do not refer to reality'. In fact, mathematics and physics operate with different rules, and should be kept apart to some extent. Physics is empirical, based on measurement, but mathematics is based on 'axioms' that are assumed at the outset.

Earlier in the twentieth century, Wittgenstein noted this perplexity, and decided, unusually for him, that it was reasonable. Pythagoras and the ancient Greeks had previously thought that even to talk of the square root of two was a heresy. People were drowned for discussing it. (The secret being that it doesn't have one. Although it does have an 'irrational' one, of course!) What they would have thought of an imaginary number really doesn't bear thinking about.

Problem 68
G. E. Moore's problem

George Edward Moore (1873–1958) was the Cambridge philosopher known for his 26-year editorship of *Mind*, probably the dullest journal in the world. His 'naturalistic fallacy' denied that the 'is' in the sentence 'pleasure is good', was a real 'is'. A real 'is' is like, for example, 'snow is white'. Moore said 'is' should only be used for 'natural' properties.

Funnily enough, years later, Moore admitted to never having given 'any tenable explanation' of what he meant by saying 'good' was not a natural property.

Problems 69–70
Kant's problem and More Kant

Immanuel Kant (1724–1804), the stern Königsberg professor of logic and metaphysics, made his most important contribution to philosophy by inventing not just one (which is enough for most professors) but *four* new terms. These were: *analytic* as opposed to *synthetic*, and *a priori* as opposed to *a posteriori*. Their meanings are extremely obscure.

The terms apply to propositions, which are special kinds of sentences which logicians think can be either true or false – ones like 'all apples are red', but definitely not 'Hello everyone!' 'Analytic' comes from the Latin, meaning 'pull apart' or 'pull asunder'. Analytic propositions are those which are true by definition, which contain 'no new information'. When 'pulled apart', they can be seen to be definitely true. Something like 'apples are apples', for example. Philosophers value these sorts of statement very highly.*

The *a priori* and *a posteriori* distinction is between things that can be known before, prior, to examining the real world, and things which can be known after, 'post', looking at it. By combining the terms, there are additional obscurities possible, notably synthetic *a priori* or synthetic *a posteriori*. Analytic *a priori* statements are necessarily true, by virtue of being tautologies. They are known by reason alone. Analytic *a posteriori* truths may not exist, but if they did, would probably be new logical truths just discovered.

Synthetic statements (from the Latin 'put together'), on the other hand, are not tautologies and do contain new information. Kant declared the whole of maths and the notion of 'cause and effect', so important for science, to be synthetic *a priori*, this on the grounds that our ability to experience anything depends already on 'causality'.

Synthetic *a posteriori* statements are the lowest of the low, things that are empirically true, in the manner of information obtained by scientists through experiments. They are frowned upon by serious philosophers.

* The determined reader may like to try 'Are There *A Priori* Concepts?' by J. L. (John Langshaw) Austin (1911–60) in *Proceedings of the Aristotelian Society*, Supplementary Volume XII, 1939.

Discussions

So what of the questions? They are clearly quite meaningless, and no one would ask them except, perhaps, if they were being paid to.

Problem 71
The table

Philosophers don't like tables. They're always calling into doubt their very existence. Bertrand Russell warns in *The Problems of Philosophy* that 'our familiar table' is actually 'a problem full of surprising possibilities'. Bishop Berkeley, for instance, says that the table is an idea in the mind of God, whilst Götfried Leibniz thinks that they are colonies of souls. Even scientists say that when we look at a table, all we see is an illusion of substance – the apparently solid object is really lots of little atoms held together by strange forces. Worse than that, they say that the atoms themselves are largely empty space, full of sub-atomic particles like electrons. And what are the particles themselves made of? 'Well,' the physicists may finish off, in a confidential whisper, 'these particles don't even really exist – they keep appearing and disappearing! Why, some of them even wait to see if they're being observed before they decide what to do!'

Particles are made up of energy, which has mass (or weight). Mass and energy can be connected – a little bit of mass goes to make a lot of energy ($E = mc^2$). A heavy object moving fast requires a lot of energy to stop it. Similarly, if harnessed, it can perform a lot of work. In the normal way, we can work out the mass of something, and calculate its speed or velocity, and deduce its momentum.

Particles, however, only have either a precise momentum (that is mass times velocity, or very loosely, size times speed) or location in space. Measure one more precisely, and the other becomes a little less certain. Measure one absolutely precisely – and the other is completely uncertain! This is known as Heisenberg's Uncertainty Principle. If it were not for this Uncertainty Principle, it would be theoretically possible for someone very clever to predict the fate of the entire universe. (Probably using a computer. Or tea leaves . . .) With the principle, everything is uncertain, open-ended possibilities. It states that you cannot know the position and the momentum of even one particle precisely. You can know either its position, or its momentum (that is, its speed or velocity multiplied by its size, or mass) but not both. At least, not both at the same time.

Einstein did not like the idea of things being uncertain, even in the sub-atomic world. So he suggested a thought experiment with a little box with a clock in it. The idea was that if a particle in the box triggers the clock, we know both where it is (in the box) at exactly what time, and can deduce its momentum. However, whilst the practical problems may be considerable, there is a worse theoretical flaw in the proposal. This is that as the particle enters or leaves the box, the box moves slightly. Not very much, but enough to mean that we don't in fact know exactly 'where' the supposed particle is after all. Its position remains uncertain.

So what is left of the table? Only an appearance of solidity, an appearance of shape, colour, texture and so on. (Especially when you bump into it.)

All this is perfectly true. We accept the physicists' word on it. But, there remains a difference between a real illusory table and an imaginary illusory one.

(See also the section 'Elementary problems of natural philosophy', especially the discussion of Problems 92 and 93.)

Problem 72
The three embryos problem

Although many philosophical problems can seem entirely abstract, and merely a form of idle amusement for would-be intellectuals, originally philosophers were practical people applying their faculties of reason to those issues that people were actually concerned about. As Epicurus (341–270 BC) said, the words of a philosopher who offers 'no therapy for human suffering' are 'empty and vain'. Contemporary philosophy has departed so far from this tradition that there is now a separate name – 'applied philosophy' – for moral discussion which seems to have some point.

Of the many issues that applied philosophy considers, those surrounding the beginnings and end of human life are the most difficult and cause some of the most bitter controversy. Some hospitals even have on their staff paid philosophers to advise doctors and surgeons just what is ethical.

This broadly medical scenario raises two separate issues: that of whether babies are in some sense 'interchangeable' so that we can swap an unsatisfactory foetus or newly born baby for another without qualms; and that of the duty the parents owe to their child to maximise its well-being.

Father Black is presumably thinking that all (human) life is sacred, and he may well be against contraception anyway. Mrs Mauve chooses to save the life of an unborn child who, it is feared, will be born with the handicap. This is to look on the foetus as more than just an object which could be swapped for a better one if desired. Mrs Brown appears to have chosen to expose her baby to an unnecessary risk, and Father Black probably only supports Mrs Brown now that she is facing the decision on abortion. His reaction to Mrs Blue's announcement that she 'will not play God' with her child seems to bear this out. Now the issue is not whether a 'potential person' is prevented from living, but simply whether the baby is given a healthy start in life or not. Mrs Blue's best chance of justifying her position to the Hospital Ethics Committee would probably be that she herself did not want the drugs, perhaps for religious reasons, as she would then be supported by the principle that every individual should be able to choose what medical treatment they do or do not receive.

Many parents in this high-tech age are asked to decide whether to abort possibly damaged foetuses, for example. It is calculated that 20 per cent of these terminations in the UK are totally erroneous anyway. Does that matter? Hospital philosophers do not necessarily have all the answers.

Problems 73–74
Kidnapped by doctors!

This analogy touches upon one devised by proponents of 'a woman's right to choose', to highlight the issue of anti-abortionists obliging women to carry through pregnancies. The proponents' point was that to insist on the woman giving up control of her body for nine months, in order to enable another human being to live, is not automatically accepted when the other human being is not an unborn baby but, say, the patient in the next bed.

This in itself is an interesting philosophical problem but, more than that, a real medical one. Likewise, the issue of consent – where patients' views may be overridden in certain circumstances – is often cropping up, particularly where the lives of others are involved. Jehovah's Witnesses may refuse to have blood transfusions, for example, and if this involves the potential death of their child, courts have in the past supported doctors in overriding the mother's wishes. This is considered less controversial for it involves not so much a physical intrusion on the patient as an affront to their beliefs.

And it could also be said to involve the protection of the interests of someone else, who is not able to consent or refuse for themself.

Philosophically speaking, a patient's change of heart, as Miss Chestnut is said to have had here, is irrelevant when the original decision was taken on the basis that another person's well-being justifies it, not that the patient is failing to recognise what is – in the experts' opinion – in their own best interests.

(These examples owe a lot to the writings of the contemporary American philosopher, Judith Jarvis Thompson.)

Problem 75
Potentially a problem

These scenarios raise all sorts of issues, about the rights of the unborn child, about the rights of the father and, of course, the rights of the mother. If we accept that in some circumstances abortion is legitimate, we may have to allow Mrs Green to 'change her mind' as in the second scenario, but we will still hesitate at the reasons suggested in the first scenario. However, a convinced utilitarian, who explains everything in terms of maximising happiness, by whatever means, might still say that the aim of the exercise is to produce the maximum amount of happiness, and that if Mrs Green is unhappy with Mr Green it is better for her to do as she plans, divorce her husband, and still bring up a baby, this time in the happy circumstances of her new relationship.

This is one of a range of problems which broadly arise from the question of when is a baby not a baby. If the embryo is a human being, then we feel it has rights, and cannot be treated in such a 'can of beans in a supermarket' sort of way. The issue of embryo 'rights' has been particularly poignant ever since 1978 when Mr and Mrs Brown (no connection with the people in our story!) in the UK successfully became the beaming parents of the world's first test-tube baby, Louise. This apparently innocuous procedure has rapidly led on to, as the technology develops, a whole raft of rather tricky ethical issues.

Whilst 'in vitro fertilisation' offers the fulfilment of family and children to many 'normal' cases, other applicants are less straightforward. What about pensioners? Lesbian or homosexual couples (or individuals)? What about heterosexual women who just prefer not to have a baby with a man? Already, some members of all these groups are having children, using the new reproductive technologies. Indeed, even people who have died are having children, as their gametes are kept in cold storage past their official 'use by' date, or are even 'rescued' following an accident. And animals are being brought into the grisly equation, as experiments in cloning are devised (the friendly looking Dolly the sheep, in the mid-1990s, for example). Animals are also being used to help scientists in their attempts to create surrogate – animal – wombs, a development which will enable men to have children without the need to locate a female partner, in much the same way as it is now possible for women to dispense with men.

The United Nations' ambitious 'Human Genome Project' catalogues the entire biological (DNA) blueprint that each cell in the human body uses to create life, and aims to enable scientists to create 'improved' versions of babies. Control of – at least – the bodily aspects of human beings is now well within the realms of scientific possibility, and the spectre of an Aldous Huxley kind of 'Brave New World', peopled by alphas (designer babies), betas (ordinary babies) and gammas (the designer babies that went wrong?) may be just around the corner.

Problem 76
Whose baby?

This is one of a snowballing number of ethical issues associated with the so-called 'new reproductive technologies'. All over the world, learned doctors and philosophers are wrestling with the issues: after all, a baby is not, as they say, 'just for Christmas'. How do you balance the internationally declared 'right to have a family', 'the rights of the unborn', the supposed rights of donors to anonymity? Perhaps the first thing to decide is just to what extent babies can or should be commodified, and produced as on a factory line, for consumers.

172

Problems 77–78

A sinister transplant problem and More sinister transplant problems

This is a variation on human organ donations, which the Trust's managers may have noted making other medical businesses a useful amount of money. Already, human kidneys are bought and sold in certain countries, typically for export to the West (where medical companies are restricted in their organ purchases) and, within the West, there are financial arrangements for the donation of male and female gametes to enable others to have children, including the surrogate use of wombs. Quite where the line should be drawn is not clear, and it is continually moved and obscured by the ever-changing technical possibilities.

Problem 79
The turtle

The turtle hasn't gone wrong at all, of course, except inasmuch as it allowed itself to be controlled by the man.

For the 'fair-minded' man is expecting to get his turtle soup without having to take moral responsibility for killing the turtle. If the turtle falls in whilst trying to do acrobatics most unsuited to its breed, he will be able to say that the turtle chose to do them. If the turtle refuses to try to cross the boiling pan of water, then he will simply knock it in and again claim that the turtle chose death rather than try to save itself through performing a simple task.

So what's the moral of the story, for us? Perhaps it is that it is better to refuse to obey a dictator than to try to please them in the hope that they will somehow respect 'the rules'.

Of course, it might not help this turtle to stand firm on its principles, but then at least the 'fair-minded' man will know that *he* hasn't got any.

(This traditional story is attributed to Cheng Shi, after Yue Ke of the twelfth or thirteenth century.)

Problem 80
The nightingale's song

When something like a beautiful orchid turns out to be made of plastic, we feel cheated. Yet in a plastic flower competition, the cheat is the one who uses real orchids instead!

Some might say that the problem is with the emperor's competition. Isn't it simply enough to be someone who sounds like a nightingale? And the answer is that indeed it is not enough.

The traditional tale talks actually of a 'pig's squeal', not a nightingale's song at all. And the point of that is to emphasise the superiority of the artist's representation over mere happenstance reality. It is not a single squeal or song that is needed, but the form of nightingale-songness (or pig-squealness).

In this sense, the competition is also about who can transcend the world of appearance to the world of the aesthete and the true philosopher. And that is why our tricky contestant rightly deserves to be thrown out of the competition.

Another fake forgery

Of course, to an expert, the difference between a fake and a forgery is simply a matter of quality. Take the sketch of *Head of a Young Girl*, by Henri Matisse, the famous French impressionist, in 1941, and the notorious fake copy, drawn with exactly the same ink, on the identical paper.

First of all, let us have a look without knowing which is which, and see which one we think is best. Superficially they look a little similar, but when you look closer you will surely see that one is shallow and lacks depth, whilst the other has a freshness and a vitality, much more than a mere doodle, it exudes character. In the words of one such arty expert:

> The copy is so inferior, so servile, that in my eyes the spirit of trickery is blatant. The hand follows the line of the master, but has not the surety, nor the rhythm, the pen cannot kiss the paper with the same gentleness.

Henri Matisse, *Tête de Jeune Fille*
© Succession H. Matisse/Archives Michel Maket.

Absolutely! The one on the right is rubbish, and lacks any 'spirit'. A crude copy indeed. If I had bought it (unknowingly), I like Lord Snooty would hide it in my attic.

Our art expert adds:

Yes, but the one you are admiring is the fake. It is the one on the right that is the original.

Ah yes! That's right! As I was saying, now I look more closely, that one has a certain sureness of style, a rhythm . . . ? The other – phooey!

Problems 81–88
Fundamentally religious problems

The 'problem' of proving God's existence is an old one in philosophy, and often the universe's existence is taken as the best – indeed the only – evidence for it. But the parishioner's first problem remains an 'unsolved one', and it is understandable if the Vicar prefers to shift the focus to consideration of the point of the universe rather than the origin.

But the next few questions are no easier, really coming down to the so-called 'Problem of evil', the problem set out in the Old Testament for Job, who finds everything begins to go wrong after God makes a bet with the Devil.

Poor Job! Through no fault of his own, his sheep and camels die, his crops fail and even his beloved children are plucked away, as the Almighty tries to test his faith. Job, of course, at first takes these misfortunes in his stride, hence the old saying about having 'the patience of Job'. But in the biblical story, the Devil pleads with God to be allowed to additionally torment Job himself with various unsavoury diseases. At which point Job's faith crumbles and he takes to railing against God and the injustice of the world.

Even though God apparently tries to make amends, restoring to Job some of his lost possessions, the story makes sadly clear that faith is easier when things go well.

Yet, by definition (as philosophers like to say – see Problem 5, 'The raven', for example – and usually without much justification) God is the maximally powerful, good-looking being that runs things in the universe. There may be disagreements amongst Her many adherents on the details, but this omnipotence characteristic all agree on. And whilst it is possible to produce a slightly convoluted explanation of why an allpowerful, maximally good being might create such a rotten world (for example, citing 'free will' or even – human arrogance – the 'laws' of physics!), there has never really been a convincing response to these questions. (Although some philosophers say we don't care about the ants' problems – so why should God care about ours?) In the Middle Ages, saintly experts such as Aurelius Augustine saw human life as essentially a rather unpleasant sort of moral trial, with the unpleasantness a necessary part of achieving saintliness. (Not to be confused with St Thomas Aquinas, famous for producing not one but five proofs of God's existence, the number in itself, perhaps, casting doubt on the Almighty.)

Conversely, it might be said, in the manner of Dr Pangloss, that we already live in the 'best of all possible worlds'. But to those of us with any fellow feeling, this seems a cruel sort of explanation.

Oriental philosophy has its own version of the problem. It starts from the fact in the world that some people are evil, or at least do evil things. It would seem to follow that either people are fundamentally evil, or they are fundamentally good but something in the world is corrupting them. Mencius (372–289 BC), the idealistic Confucian philosopher, held the latter view of humanity (as did Plato, who made education the keystone in his philosophy), and said that culture and education were at fault. But the problem arose that as both things are essentially human artefacts, how can fundamentally good people produce something so corrupting?

And the reverse position, put by Hsun Tzu (313–238 BC), a generation later, that (unfortunately) people are basically wicked, but through education and social pressure we can change them for the better, also begs the question of why something good should emerge from something bad.

Actually, a fairly easy solution to this problem would be to suppose that people are a mixture of good and bad. This has the advantage of being in harmony with the Chinese principle of the dynamic balance of all creation, between yin and yang, being and not being, good and evil. Even the most wicked person is capable of doing something good, after all.

The later problems are more concerned with what, to modern ears, sounds like the rather archaic notion of souls. Yet the word is important. If there is 'no such thing', as many self-consciously 'modern' materialists would say, then what is it that makes people special – better than animals – or machines? The parishioner raises some quite genuine problems for the Vicar, and the latter's remark about 'communicating' is not such a bad point from which to start answering the questions.

As William James might have put it, science and religion are really two slices of bread, with philosophy in the middle. Scientists reduce the world to 'matter', make the world into a machine and destroy free will, and purpose. Philosophies which instead reduce matter to mind, allow for us to have a purpose and the freedom to find it are really religions.

Problem 89
The evangelist

The scenario, although bizarre, is in fact based on an actual legal case involving a witch doctor in a UK colony, tried for murder in the 1950s after arrest and transportation to Britain, related by Anthony Kenny. In the actual case, following the discovery of the harmlessness of the witch doctor's potion, the court transmuted the death sentence to a prison term.

In our story, the Reverend appears to have deliberately worried some people, with the rather extreme result that they become ill and die. If the worry had been, for example, about overeating, then we would certainly feel he should be held at least partly responsible. Given the element that it is a worry that only affects people who feel they have been bad, and the solution is apparently being offered, even a prison sentence seems rather harsh.

Problem 90
Poincaré's problem

The French philosopher-mathematician, Jules-Henri Poincaré, takes up the story:

'A moving object will become smaller and smaller as it approaches the circumference of the sphere. Let us observe, in the first place, that although from the point of view of our geometers this world is finite, to its inhabitants it will appear infinite.'

Henri's point is a simple one. Nothing in the story is against the rules of logic, however unlikely given our everyday experiences of nature. Yet it appears to show that the assumptions of the truths of geometry, indeed the laws of the universe, are not beyond doubt. The gaseous people say that their planet is infinite, and as they can never step outside it, for them it is. Yet from the perspective of any passing space traveller, they are living an illusion.

The ancient Greek geometers left a legacy of respect for the eternal truths of their science, and the certainty of their truths. Yet do the angles of a triangle always add up to 180°? Is it really certain that parallel lines never meet? Only if we assume that space is flat.

Jules-Henri Poincaré's answer to Jeometers and geometers alike is the same: no measurements can be said to be the 'real ones' – it is all just a matter of convention.

See also: *Wittgenstein's Beetle (and other Classic Thought Experiments)* (Martin Cohen, Blackwell, 2005) which includes a picture of the ladder!

Problem 91
Problems with the speed of light

Scientists, especially astronomers, have been measuring the speed of light for a long time. Galileo (1564–1642) sent an assistant up nearby Italian hills to flick signals across to him using shuttered lanterns in an early, brave but futile, bid to see how long it took light to travel the distance. (He was thwarted by the variable reaction speeds of even the most attentive assistant.)

A century later, the Danish astronomer Olaf Roemer did slightly better, by increasing the distance light had to travel by millions of miles, and using the moons of Jupiter as a yardstick, at which point he observed it seemed to take an eminently measurable amount of time.

This proved that light definitely had a speed. It didn't say anything about it always travelling at the same one, which was altogether more unexpected. But, despite the simple technology, Michelson and Morley correctly identified the defining principle of modern physics. Light always travels at the same speed through space. (It goes a bit slower through liquids, and it can also be affected by gravity, particularly nastily by black holes.) Einstein's theories of relativity only 'rediscovered' this fact. From this experiment followed a number of important things, not least the relativity of time and space.

It may seem silly that light can do this. But suppose we are, as a galaxy, accelerating away from another galaxy at three-quarters of the speed of light – and we *are* doing this from some of them. Then suppose there is another galaxy, diametrically opposite and further away still, and accelerating away from the middle one at just a weeny bit under a quarter of the speed of light. Now, if the velocities could be added together, as most velocities can, then one day the third, most distant, galaxy would appear to just 'go out' suddenly and disappear, the combined velocities having exceeded the maximum speed of light and the light waves no longer being able to get to us. And that would be almost as silly as light always travelling at the same speed. Although we see a lot of remarkable things in the sky – we do not see galaxies blinking out.

Problems 92–93
Further problems of natural philosophy and Advanced further problems of natural philosophy

The 'Two slits experiment', as it is sometimes known, is one of the perplexing, untidy threads of science that indicates everything in the world is not as simple as we sometimes imagine. It was first carried out as long ago as 1803 by Thomas Young, using sunlight, and it shows that 'Newtonian mechanics', which is the way we tend to believe the world works (ever since magical explanations fell out of fashion), really only explains a bit about why apples fell on Sir Isaac as he dreamt under the tree.

The experiment indicates that the fundamental Newtonian notion of 'predictability', given 'starting conditions', does not seem to apply to particles of energy. Even if we know the speed of the particles, where they start from and the direction of travel, we cannot tell what is going to happen. In the case of the 'Two slits experiment', we need to know an extra piece of information: is the other one open?

One contemporary physicist, Henry Stapp, put it this way: how can the particle know about the other slit anyway? Indeed, how can everything in the universe know about everything else – instantly?

Einstein, concerned as ever about the apparent 'untidiness' of the universe, disputed the inferences other scientists made. One, perhaps more 'rational', explanation offered for the apparent ability of light to behave as both waves and particles, is that the packets of energy that photons are thought to be spin in certain directions. This motion enables particles to cancel each other out in the manner of a wave, where one spinning clockwise cancels out one spinning anti-clockwise, for example. But it still doesn't help explain how a single photon can behave in a wave-like way, as the second problem shows.

So, most physicists these days talk of 'probability waves', as opposed to 'real waves' like those of liquids. Probability waves have no fixed spatial qualities, just a tendency to appear in certain locations. This allows a photon to not be tied down to choosing one slit to travel through. But as soon as we know which slit the photon has gone through (and we do know once the detector is placed there) the possibility of it going through the other slit is reduced to nil. In the quantum (very small amounts) world, particles seem to behave differently when observed. The observer affects the observation. Which leads on to . . .

Problem 94
Schrödinger's cat's problem

Well, some physicists have suggested that the best thing to do would be to put a human being in the box. The idea is that they could then observe the particle directly, and thus prevent the 'uncertainty' arising. This, in a funny way, comes back to a much older philosophical debate, that the reality of anything depends on it being observed. The physicists Eugene Wigner and John Wheeler, for example, have recently advanced this explanation of sub-atomic phenomena. Wigner even thinks that the solution to the 'mind/body problem' is to be found in quantum physics.

This is the view summed up by Bishop George Berkeley in the eighteenth century, as *esse est percipi* (Latin for 'to be is to be perceived'). Philosophers speculated about whether if a tree fell over in a forest it made any sound if there was no one around to hear it. But the tree doesn't need to fall over to have its 'existence' called into question. If there is no one there to see it, or smell it . . . ?

Similarly, today some physicists speculate over whether the cat is capable of perceiving the events in the box, and thereby forcing the particle to either exist or not exist, and trigger its own demise or not. Some of them say that, at the very least, the cat knows whether it is alive or not! But this is actually a particularly doubtful rejoinder – even human beings, however good we may be at knowing we are alive, may have difficulty knowing the reverse!

Berkeley's reply to his detractors was that everything existed after all, because God perceived everything.

This comfortable notion led to the penning of two limericks:

> There once was a man who said 'God
> Must think it exceedingly odd
> If he finds that this tree
> Continues to be
> When there's no one about in the Quad.'

> Dear Sir, Your astonishment's odd
> I am always about in the Quad
> And that's why the tree
> Will continue to be
> Since observed by, Yours faithfully, God.

Problem 95
The space yacht's black hole

Well, no, the universe can cope even with Mr Megasoft's space yachts. The problem is a bit like that signalled all those years ago in Zeno's paradox of 'Achilles and the tortoise'. For the stars behind the spaceship, Mr Megasoft is in the position of the tortoise in the race. The light has a lot of catching up to do. Now if the spaceship was going at a constant speed, as today's spaceships do after their initial burst of acceleration, the light would indeed catch up, whatever the logic of Zeno's argument. But as the spaceship is accelerating all the time, by the time the light has got halfway to where the ship was, it finds the ship is now going faster, so the next bit of catching up is harder. At a certain point the light can never catch up, even though the spaceship is *still* going slower than the lightwaves chasing after it.

Problems 96–97
Schopenhauer's problem and Schopenhauer's problem too

These two problems are not respectable and not normally discussed of course. Philosophers don't like sex. It is, after all, highly irrational. Plato (in *The Republic*, Book III, 403) even had Socrates ask his friend Glaucon, in his usual rhetorical manner, whether 'true love can have any contact with frenzy or excess of any kind?' The answer Glaucon gives obligingly is, most certainly not, but Socrates, unusually, goes on to spell it out.

SOCRATES: True love can have no contact with this sexual pleasure, and lovers whose love is true must neither of them indulge in it.
GLAUCON: They certainly must not, Socrates.
SOCRATES: And so, I suppose you will lay down laws in the state we are founding [planning] that will allow a lover to associate with his boy-friend and kiss him and touch him, if he permits it, as a father does his son, if his motives are good; but require that his association with anyone he's fond of must never give rise to the least suspicion of anything beyond this, otherwise he will be thought a man of no taste or education.
GLAUCON: That is how I should legislate.

But Arthur Schopenhauer – who really did exist, and really was called Arthur (it being a useful, even cosmopolitan, name for a career in European business) – is surely right. The reproductive urge, be it simply the sexual one or be it the more respectable procreative one, is so strong, it is somehow fundamental and really philosophers are being a bit evasive if they continue to discuss the nature of human life without any reference at all to it. At least Plato did value a sort of filial love, the kind ever since called 'Platonic'. Unfortunately, the Christian Church taught a rather extreme version of the doctrine for most of the millennia between Socrates and Schopenhauer, which culminated in the most bizarre and hypocritical attitudes towards sex. (A point made by the twentieth-century French philosopher Michel Foucault [1926–84].)

It could be said that Schopenhauer was simply reflecting two unfortunate experiences. One was being sent to boarding school in Wimbledon, and the other was giving his first lecture in philosophy at the same time as his celebrated contemporary, Professor Hegel. Hardly anyone came to Schopenhauer's talk, and he so bitterly resented the fact that he swore never to give a public lecture again. On the other hand, as Aristotle wrote in the *Nicomachean Ethics*, 'without friends, no one would choose to live, though he had all other goods'.

Problem 98
A fairly terminal problem for dull philosophers

Biggles uses logic

In one of Captain W. E. Johns' famous storybooks, the heroic fighter ace, Biggles, uses cool logic to explain his indifference to risk:

> When you are flying, everything is all right or it is not all right. If it is all right there is no need to worry. If it is not all right one of two things will happen. Either you will crash or you will not crash. If you do not crash there is no need to worry. If you do crash one of two things is certain. Either you will be injured or you will not be injured. If you are not injured there is no need to worry. If you are injured one of two things is certain. Either you will recover or you will not recover. If you recover there is no need to worry. If you don't recover you can't worry.

> (From W. E. Johns, *Spitfire Parade*, 1941)

The formulation sounds very useful, and philosophers have long sought to reduce complex moral and ethical issues into logical form, all the better to proclaim on them. If this can be done, a machine – such as a computer – can quickly whirr through the possible permutations before delivering a nice tidy answer. Leibniz indeed sketched some ideas for just such a computational device and dreamt of the day when philosophers would announce to each other 'Come, let us calculate,' rather than fall out over issues.

The first step is putting the problem into the language of formal logic, which attempts to follow certain 'rules of reasoning' drawn up by Aristotle – a long time ago. There are many practical reasons why this is difficult, and a few theoretical ones too. Not least that in order to achieve logical form, the eventual conclusion must be assumed at the outset. Notwithstanding this, logicians carry on their convoluted and frequently indigestible linguistic acrobatics.

But some slightly ridiculous consequences have to be swallowed already even with this fairly modest beginning. The first is that any argument with inconsistent premises is valid, irrespective of what the conclusions of that argument are. For example:

Dogs always have tails
Some dogs do not have tails
The moon is made of green cheese

is an example of a philosophically valid argument.

'Dogs always have tails' is the first premise, and the second is that 'Some dogs do not have tails.' It follows logically that the moon is made of green cheese, because anything at all follows from inconsistent premises. This is because there will never be an occasion when both the premises are true, and the conclusion false (the only way for such a piece of reasoning to be 'invalid'), because there will never be an occasion when the premises are true. (And it may not be so obvious that the premises are inconsistent!)

Another logical curiosity is the case of an argument with a conclusion that is necessarily true.

Money grows on trees
The King of the Potato People likes money
Money is either a good thing or a bad thing or neither

. . . is again perfectly 'valid'.

Here the argument is valid irrespective of what the premises are. This is because there are no circumstances in which the conclusion can be false, and the premises true, because the conclusion itself cannot be false. So if our conclusion is that 'Money is either a good thing or a bad thing or neither', we can advance as 'evidence' the fact that 'money grows on trees' and 'the King of the Potato People likes money', and still have our argument considered 'valid'.

Finally, 'If cats can fly, then dogs can drive cars', is a perfectly valid inference, as a false statement implies any statement whatsoever. This is because the only way 'If first thing then something else' can be falsified is by finding a situation where the 'first thing' is true yet the 'something else' is false, which cannot ever happen here.

So making our arguments logically valid doesn't reliably tell us anything about our conclusion, and can be very misleading.

(This is also discussed in the Glossary.)

Problem 99
Descartes' big problem

The answer is, of course, you don't. It seems unlikely that either you're dreaming, or suspended in a vat of chemicals (or both, as happens at some health clubs) but then computers of today are getting very sophisticated (and demons always have been). Anyway, we only know it's unlikely by referring to other experiences that we've already had, all of which may have been made-up tricks too.

In fact, as René Descartes famously observed whilst curled up in an old French stone oven (and as we saw in Problem 2), there's only one thing that anyone can be sure of, and that's that there are thoughts. You can't be 'tricked' into thinking you are thinking, because the trick still requires your thinking. *Cogito ergo sum*, as it goes in Latin – 'I think therefore I am.' Although, the 'I' in this can't be taken too literally, to refer to anyone in particular – only to a 'thinking thing'.

This one certain truth, from which Descartes deduced the rest of the world, might better be translated as 'There is a thinking thing thinking things.' Or then again, maybe not.

Anyway, who is the 'thinking thing'? No one knows for sure. Perhaps it's God.

Problem 100
The problem of how to get to 101 (unsolved)

Or is it a problem with existence? A problem with our 'conceptual spectacles' (as some philosophers would have it – conceptual blinkers more like, others might add) which colour everything we see, distorting and disguising?

Plato and most of the ancient Greeks certainly didn't think so. They considered the activity of idly discussing issues that no one knew the answers to, and were pretty sure they weren't going to find out either, to be one of the highest activities of 'the rational animal', of humankind. Of course, they had to rely on a slave society to create the leisure time of the philosophising classes. But the Eastern tradition of sages and monks is less exploitative, and just as impractical. Indeed, it is from the mystic tradition that much of Greek philosophy stems, and with it ideas of harmony, souls and reincarnation.

Discussions

Étienne Bonnot de Condillac (1715–80) tells the following story. Imagine waking from a deep sleep and finding yourself in a labyrinth together with some other people who are busy arguing over general principles for finding the way out. What, Étienne exclaims, could appear more ridiculous! Yet that, he says, is what the philosophers are doing. 'It is more important to find ourselves merely where we were at first than to believe prematurely that we are out of the labyrinth', he concludes.

But the other approach, as suggested by the problem itself, is that we have better things to do than meditate. These days we want to do things, make things, achieve things. These days we deal practically with the world, using machines that are better tools than our bodies, indeed better tools than our minds. No one ever got rich by meditating, after all.

And philosophy has moved with the times, too. The spectacular breakthroughs in technical innovation that were achieved in the nineteenth and twentieth centuries spawned their own philosophical movement – that of the Logical Positivists of the Vienna Circle in the inter-war years.

The Circle would only admit those who agreed that nothing anyone says has any meaning unless it can be checked up on using scientific procedures of 'verification'. Philosophers, of course, are still very important, as they can check that the verified claims and indeed the unverified ones, are expressed nice and logically.

The 'hub' of this circle, Moritz Schlick, decried the view that 'the final and perhaps the most important truths' are permanently hidden from our eyes; that 'the key to the Riddle of the Universe is buried'. He put it this way in an article for *The Philosopher* in 1936. Evidently, he agrees, there are unanswerable questions:

> It is very easy to ask questions the answers to which, we have the strongest reasons to believe, will never be known to any human being. What did Plato do at eight o'clock in the morning of his fiftieth birthday? How much did Homer weigh when he wrote the first line of the Iliad? Is there a piece of silver to be found on the other side of the moon, three inches long and shaped like a fish? Obviously, men will never know the answers to these questions, however hard they may try. But at the same time, we know that they would never try very hard. These problems, they will say, are of no importance, no philosopher would worry about them, and no historian or naturalist would care whether he knew the answers or not.

Unfortunately, Moritz Schlick goes on, concerned that some of the most important issues of philosophy are also generally held to belong to the class of insoluble problems, either 'logically' unanswerable, in principle, or 'empirically' unanswerable, due to practical circumstances. But no real question should be logically unanswerable. For that would be equivalent to not being able to indicate its meaning, and a question which has no meaning is not a question at all: just a 'nonsensical series of words with a question mark after them'.

Thus, Professor Schlick roundly concludes, when a philosopher confounds us with a series of words like 'What is the nature of Time?' or 'Can we know the Absolute?' and 'neglects to explain their meaning by careful and accurate explanation and definitions', they cannot wonder when no answer is forthcoming. 'It is as if they had asked us: "How much does philosophy weigh?" It is not a question at all, but mere nonsense.'

You can see the approach of the Logical Positivists owes at least some small ideological debt to the unfashionable, but canny, Scottish philosopher David Hume. Hume it was who had written nearly 200 years earlier in *An Enquiry Concerning Human Understanding* (1748):

If we take in our hand any volume of divinity or school metaphysics, for instance, let us ask, *Does it contain any abstract reasoning concerning quantity or number?* No. *Does it contain any experimental reasoning concerning matters of fact and existence?* No. Commit it then to the flames: for it can contain nothing but sophistry and illusion.

But that seems a shame, particularly when you think it might even include this book.

Problem 101
The problem of existence

It used to be considered the job of the churches to solve problems about the point of existence, but these days the question 'What is the meaning of life?' is included in many exams for philosophy degrees, sometimes as a bit of light relief. However, the issue also arises in a very real form in medical ethics, particularly with the cases of the chronically ill or the very old. It seems ironic but, for too many people, the only time the question of the meaning of life is taken seriously is when it's almost over.

So what is the point of it all anyway? Schopenhauer, as we saw in Problems 96 and 97, was convinced he had stumbled upon the answer: sex. Not that he means it quite like *that*. More he meant the answer lies in the drive, the prompting of our genetic code to successfully reproduce itself, sculpted by countless millennia of evolution. In the *World as Will and Representation*, he writes:

> The earth rolls on from day into night; the individual dies; but the sun itself burns without intermission, an eternal noon. Life is certain to the will-to-live; the form of life is endless present; it matters not how individuals, the phenomenal of the Idea, arise and pass away in time, like fleeting dreams.

Many writers these days repeat this theory, using different terms, always hoping to appear very dry and scientific. One such (Stuart Kaufman) says the point is to be 'self-reproducing and do at least one thermo-dynamic work-cycle', but we still don't have to accept this solution to the problem. There are alternatives, some very materialistic, some very idealistic. The latter kind may be that life is about truth and beauty and goodness, and coming to know it. That's certainly what Socrates taught. And that, in one way or another, is what all the problems in this book are about. At the same time, some Eastern philosophies warn that even these are just 'concepts', and lack ultimate reality.

Anyway, many more people, some in ancient Greece, favour answers of the materialistic kind – answers along the lines of 'to have fun', 'to get rich', 'to become world dictator', and so on. But if life is about the 'pursuit of happiness' – what if we aren't very good at it? Most of us, most of the time, seem not to be. In fact, the central problem of Buddhism is overcoming suffering in the world. Philolaus of Croton (c.479–390 BC) gloomily puts it in the *Miscellanies*, that the soul has been yoked to the body as a punishment and it is 'imprisoned within it as though in a tomb'. On the other hand, Buddhism is very practical: eating and sleeping are seen as part of being and are considered important, even whilst individuals may strive to attain an ability to accept hardship when needed. For Buddhists, the answer to questions about the point of life, the universe and everything, is that the point just *is* life, the universe and everything.

But some might not be satisfied with this, and (unwilling for the book to finish) ask whether, perhaps, just a few lucky people have any *real* point, and the rest of us act just as some kind of necessary but rather unappealing by-product.

Friedrich Nietzsche, born in the Prussian town of Röcken into a decade that saw uprisings and revolutions all over Europe, certainly seemed to think so. Nietzsche saw human beings, and indeed all life, as engaged in a struggle to increase their *power*.

Nietzsche was a philosopher-poet who wrote of 'Supermen' and battles, of 'the will to power', and of magnificent destinies. Yet Nietzsche, the historical man, was a rather less dashing figure, prone to ill-health, headaches, chronic short-sight and intestinal problems, unattractive to the opposite sex despite a voracious sexual appetite, cutting, in many ways, a tragic figure, the opposite of what he would have wanted.

Nietzsche's intention, declaring himself the 'first immoralist', 'proud to possess this word which sets me off against the whole of humanity' (thereby neglecting for example François, Duc de la Rochefoucauld [1613–80] who had written: 'Nobody deserves to be praised for goodness unless he is strong enough to be bad, for any other goodness is usually merely inertia or lack of will'). His hope was to 'revalue' all values, starting with the unmasking of Christianity and literally making 'good' 'bad', but this task was never completed. Instead, *Ecce Homo*, 'Behold the Man', a semi-blasphemous title in itself, has to stand as his definitive work for, early in 1889, he descended into a twilight of his own, never emerging from madness. The book's conclusion was supposed to be an ode to his own excellence, but it is actually an anthem to the German interpretation of fascism.

> The concept 'God' invented as the antithetical concept in life – everything harmful, noxious, slanderous, the whole mortal enmity against life brought into one terrible unity! The concept 'the Beyond', 'real world' invented so as to deprive of value the only world which exists – so as to leave over no goal, no reason, no task for our earthly reality! The concept 'soul', 'spirit', finally even 'immortal soul', invented so as to despise the body, so as to make it sick – 'holy' – so as to bring to all the things in life which deserve serious attention, the question of nutriment, residence, cleanliness, weather, a horrifying frivolity! . . . Finally, it is the most fateful, in the concept of the good man common cause made with everything weak, sick, ill-constituted, suffering from itself, all that which ought to perish – the law of selection crossed, an ideal made of opposition to the proud and well-constituted, to the affirmative man, to the man certain of the future and guaranteeing the future.*

Discussions

(Incredibly, Nietzsche is much admired in trendy, liberal circles these days.) Nietzsche wrote too, that the goal of humanity is not in some supposed general strategy or process, such as the maximisation of happiness, but is to be found in the activities of its 'highest specimens'. These men (and it is only *men*) transcend history, and are bound to no laws other than that of their own pleasure. In *The Will to Power*, he tries to explain behaviour for the whole of nature as power-seeking, even including plants and rocks.

This all reflected Nietzsche's early interests in the contests of the ancient Greeks, where life was indeed a series of contests, for the strong in athletics or fighting, for musicians and poets, and even for philosophers, such as Socrates. In Nietzsche's eyes, Socrates was in fact a very powerful man, second only to Heraclitus, the aristocrat from Ephesus (nicknamed 'the Dark'), whom Nietzsche claims as a fellow believer in the 'joy' of destruction: 'destruction, the decisive element in Dionysian philosophy, affirmation of antithesis and war, *becoming* with a radical rejection even of the concept of "being"'.

---

* Nietzsche 1889: 133–34, edited by R. J. Hollingdale, Penguin edition, 1979.

Nietzsche applies his theory of power to history, and makes some illuminating new interpretations. The 'Superman', or *Übermensch*, is for Nietzsche the logical outcome of his theory, an individual enjoying his power to the full, untrammelled by notions of justice or pity. And we might usefully substitute the word 'money' for 'power' (after all, money is the embodiment of power), to see how widespread this notion is.

Philosophically, Nietzsche represents an extreme case of the apparently innocuous view that there is no meaning to life except that which individuals can create for themselves. The only way out of this futility and meaninglessness is through action and creation – and the purest forms of these are through the exercise of power.* Whereas conventional teaching, epitomised by Christianity but also so strongly advanced by Socrates, would have it that people should be good, and through being good comes happiness. Nietzsche argues that this is the 'slave morality' and is born out of guilt, weakness and resentment, with good only a shadow form of the absence of resentment.

Other, more respectable, humanist challenges to religion dispute its claim that the point of being alive is to please or serve God. Or indeed to get to heaven. Logically, it would seem, either God doesn't exist, or does and is quite capable of carrying on without being pleased or served by anyone. (It would be a very odd arrangement otherwise, really, when you think about it, as the parishioner might remark to the Vicar. And what would be the use of eternal life when we got there anyway . . . ?)

On the other hand, well-intentioned but bland platitudes about 'helping people', or the more general humanist task of increasing happiness, suffer the at least logical flaw of simply seeming to pass on the task of having a reason for being alive to the person being helped. If everyone's role is simply to help each other, wouldn't it be easier to have no one in the world at all, and no help needed?

---

* Nietzsche's sense of the pointlessness of life was added to by his version of the Greek theory of 'eternal recurrence', in which the universe, in an early kind of Cosmic Big Bang, circles round a predetermined physical cycle, with everything, including ourselves, coming and going in and out of existence with it. Apparently, fairly basic mathematics shows that even if there are only a few atoms in a finite space, they can configure and reconfigure themselves for an infinitely long period of time without, happily, having to repeat any pattern exactly.

All the explanations seem to come back to the unpalatable truth that there really *isn't* any point at all to human existence. Or is it only that the point *is* simply to carry on, as T. S. Eliot puts it in *The Cocktail Party*, one of his post-modern, angst-ridden plays? As Titus Lucretius Carus warned, in the first century BC, against forgetting that there are bounds to both accumulation and to pleasure, and allowing 'malign dissatisfaction', to 'sweep life out to sea'. Perhaps we should stop worrying about not existing. But then why, if there isn't any point to existing, do we have such a strong biological prompting to avoid dying? More than that, why are we so sad when (at least some) other people die?

People (they wouldn't want to call themselves philosophers) who put forward scientific explanations (like the genetic one) are offering things that are not really explanations at all. They are merely descriptions of mechanisms. To explain how we see by saying light stimulates the receptors of the retina is simply to put the question of how we see back one stage. (How does stimulating the receptors of the retina make us see?) To explain the purpose of human existence by saying it is to reproduce, is simply to describe the mechanism of existence. You might as well say the purpose of being alive is eating. (Which almost brings us back to the Buddhists again and, actually . . .)

It is with problems like these that philosophy comes into its own and enables us to look into the dreadful chasm, the silent abyss of the insoluble – hopefully without falling in. After all, if we weren't here, the universe wouldn't be either.

Or would it?

Glossary

This is a (largely) alphabetical glossary of terms and people mentioned in the text, giving additional background information, and offered here as a kind of philosophical 'toolbox'. However, it is not intended to be either a comprehensive survey, or an impartial one. Readers wanting to delve deeper will still wish to go on to some of the sorts of book mentioned in the Reading Guide at the end of the book.

Philosophy Philosophy is the subject of this book. It is sometimes misleadingly defined as 'the love of wisdom', from the Greek *philia*, love, and *sophia*, wisdom. Some people say it began with the Greeks, a couple of centuries before the birth of Christ, but this would be to ignore the subtlety and insights of the Indian and Chinese traditions in particular. However, if we accept a narrower definition of philosophy for a moment, it might more accurately be paraphrased as the love of contradictions. These are obtained by creating artificially rigid distinctions, starting from the fundamental 'is/is not' one, central to Eastern philosophy. Actually, philosophers like to split *everything* into two. Moving on from 'is/is not', they go to 'true/false', 'good/bad' and, increasingly these days, to the dull distinctions of linguistic philosophy: 'subject/predicate', 'objective/subjective', 'formal/informal', 'content/context' and so on. Predicates can then be conjoined with propositions, etc., etc.

Plato termed those who used to baffle others through empty tricks with words as 'sophists', and philosophy is also the love of sophistry. But there is another sense in which the word philosophy can be used, and that is something to do with the search for values and human meanings.

Applied Philosophy Applied Philosophy is the application of philosophical techniques to real questions, for which some sort of an answer is required – for example, the sort of question which arises when medical resources are being allocated, or the various demands of the environment versus the needs of people are considered, or when business practices and profits are in conflict. It is still considered by many self-consciously serious philosophers as 'not really philosophy'. For them, the more remote their discussion is from the everyday world, the better. But some bizarre consequences can follow from this attitude. One remarkable discussion (originally penned in 1957, at the time of the great uprising in the American Civil Rights movement, and reprinted as recently as 1984) discussed, apparently oblivious to the offensiveness of the example, 'the proposition all Negroes are men'. Quoting Francis Herbert Bradley, the celebrated nineteenth-century 'idealist', John Passmore explained helpfully that the proposition seems to claim that 'the judgment ascribes an ideal content to the sign system of reality'. He goes on:

> 'All Negroes are men' asserts that Reality is such that *Negroes are human* [Passmore's italics]. It unifies by ascribing a predicate to a single Reality, although this predicate is itself a diversified one, as all propositions, ultimately, have the same form – they assert an ideal content of Reality.*

Given such total disengagement from the world everyone else lives in, applied philosophy is a welcome return to a more socially aware type of philosophy.

Glossary

Aristotle Aristotle was born in 384 BC, just in time to know Plato, and he worked on every subject under the sun with alarming taxonomical zeal. Substantial amounts of his labours have survived, and been very influential historically, but he actually wrote even more than this, including some apparently very lively dialogues in the manner of his illustrious predecessor. None of these has survived, leaving only a dry pseudoscientific collection of notes and theories. Despite or perhaps because of this, throughout the Middle Ages no other thinker had as great an influence, and he merited in the thirteenth century alone some five separate papal bans.

Neither Aristotle nor the other Greek philosophers made any distinction between scientific and philosophical investigations. Aristotle was particularly interested in observing nature, and his studies of biology were much admired by Darwin amongst others. Aristotle influenced subsequent studies by his view that organisms had a function, were striving towards some purposeful end, and that nature is not haphazard. If plant shoots are observed to bend towards the sun they are 'seeking the light'. The function of mankind is, he suggests, to reason, as this is what people are better at than any other member of the animal kingdom – 'Man is a rational animal.' This view is in contrast to the biologist or scientist who tries to explain things by reference to 'mechanisms', as if they really explain anything.

* *A Hundred Years of Philosophy*, John Passmore, Penguin, 1957, reprinted 1984, pp. 158–59.

Aristotle's greatest achievement is generally supposed to have been his Laws of Reasoning – formal logic – which, although in a sense not philosophy at all, is closely related to it. Like many contemporary philosophers he regarded logic as providing the key to philosophical progress. The traditional 'laws of thought' are that:

- whatever is, is (the law of identity);
- nothing can both be and not be (the law of non-contradiction); and
- everything must either be or not be (the law of excluded middle).

Naturally, no one agrees on any of these, but they sound good dropped into conversations.

Then there is the *Nicomachean Ethics*, one of the most influential books of moral philosophy, including accounts of what the Greeks considered to be the great virtues, and Aristotle's great-souled man, who speaks with a deep voice and level utterance, and who is not unduly modest either. The main idea in the *Ethics* is that the proper end of mankind is the pursuit of *eudaimonia*, which is Greek for a very particular kind of 'happiness'. *Eudaimonia* has three aspects: as well as mere pleasure, there is political honour, and the rewards of contemplation. Quintessentially, of course, philosophy.

Aristotle sees the soul as a kind of 'life principle' or 'life force', inseparable from the body. In the last book of *De anima*, Aristotle writes:

> Mind as we have described it is what it is by virtue of becoming all things, while there is another which is what it is by virtue of making all things: this is a sort of positive state like light; for in a sense light makes potential colours into actual colours. Mind in this sense of it is separable, impassable, unmixed. . . . When mind is set free from its present conditions it appears as just what it is and nothing more; this alone is immortal and eternal (we do not however remember its former activity, because while mind in this sense is impassable, mind as passive is destructible) and without it nothing thinks.

This passage has caused subsequent translators and commentators many problems. Dan O'Connor, one of the latter, says that it is fair to say no one knows what it means. St Thomas Aquinas has identified the intellect with the Christian 'immortal soul', whilst others have said it is God.

Aristotle was responsible for the Christian dogma that the earth was at the centre of the universe, and absolutely motionless. The universe had no beginning in time either (it would have been unacceptably sudden and rather jarring), and is spatially finite, a perfectly harmonious contraption of rotating spheres, the moon on the next one up, the firmament on the outer. In fact, most of the history of science has been untangling Aristotle's view from the observable facts. Bertrand Russell, despite or perhaps because of being a logician, had little time for the master. Writing in *An Outline of Intellectual Rubbish*, he says:

> Aristotle, in spite of his reputation, is full of absurdities. He says that children should be conceived in the Winter, when the wind is in the North, and that if people marry too young the children will be female. He tells us that the blood of females is blacker than that of males; that the pig is the only animal liable to measles; that an elephant suffering from insomnia should have its shoulders rubbed with salt, olive-oil, and warm water; that women have fewer teeth than men, and so on. Nevertheless, he is considered by the great majority of philosophers a paragon of wisdom.

Berkeley Bishop George Berkeley (1685–1753) wrote, in the *Principles of Human Knowledge*, that

> upon the whole, I am inclined to think that the greater part, if not all, of those difficulties which have hitherto amused philosophers, and blocked up the way to knowledge, are entirely owing to ourselves – that we have first of all raised up a dust and then complain that we cannot see.

Not to be outdone, the good bishop devised the doctrine that *esse est percipi*, 'to be is to be perceived', in other words, that material objects – everything – exists only through being perceived by conscious beings. To the objection that in that case, a tree, for instance, in a forest, would cease to exist when no one was around, he replied that God always perceived everything. In his opinion, this was a weighty argument.

Berkeley's main writings were penned whilst in his twenties: *A New Theory of Vision* in 1709, *The Principles of Human Knowledge* a year later and the *Dialogues of Hylas and Philonous* in 1713. In this last, his argument against matter is set out best. Hylas stands for scientific common sense, and Philonous for Berkeley's own view. After some amiable remarks, in the manner of Plato and Socrates, Hylas says he has heard that his friend holds the view that there is no such thing as matter. Can anything be more fantastical, more repugnant to common sense or a more manifest piece of scepticism, than this, he exclaims!

Philonous tries to explain that sense-data are in fact mental, as is shown by considering lukewarm water. Put a cold hand in it and it appears warm – put a hot hand in it and it appears cold. Hylas accepts this point, but clings to other sensible qualities. Philonous then says that tastes are either pleasant or unpleasant, and are therefore mental, and the same can be said of smells. Hylas valiantly rallies at this point, and says that sounds are known to not travel through a vacuum. From this, he concludes, they must be motions of air molecules, not mental entities. Philonous responds that if this is indeed real sound, it bears no resemblance to what we know as sound, so that in that case, sound may as well be considered the mental phenomenon after all. The same argument fells Hylas when it comes to a discussion of colours, which it is realised disappear under certain conditions, such as when a golden cloud at sunset is seen close up to be just a grey mist.

Likewise, size varies depending on the observer's position. Here Hylas suggests that the object should be distinguished from the perception – the act of perceiving is after all mental, but there is still a material object. Philonous replies, 'Whatever is immediately perceived is an idea: and can any idea exist out of the mind?' In other words, for something to be perceived, there must be a mind somewhere perceiving it. Why, even Hylas' brain, Philonous suggests, 'being only a sensible thing', as Hylas says, 'exists only in the mind'!

Berkeley's conclusion is that there are logical grounds for holding the view that only minds and mental events can exist. This view was adopted by Hegel and subsequent philosophers.

Colours Poor old colours – always 'subjective', always having secondary status in philosophical knowledge, trailing behind things like 'shape' or 'extension' and 'size' – even weight (which surely is very subjective . . .).

Sometimes, discussion has compared perception of colour with perception of 'pain' or indeed pleasure, and taste or smell. One way of resolving the issue of the proper status of colours for some philosophers has been to deny that colours really exist at all. Things appear to have colours, but this is misleading. Another idea is that things appear to have colours but only in relation to a perceiver. Snow is white only when someone is there to see it as white. Finally, there is the reassuring view that things really are coloured, in that they have certain 'physical properties' which we sense in the same way we sense weight, and so on.

The exact status and nature of colour perhaps help explain how David Hume got himself into such a tangle with his thought experiment on the colour blue: the so - called 'Blue Shades'. 'Suppose some one has seen many colours' says Hume, 'but never one particular shade of blue.' Then,

> let all the different shades of that colour, except that single one, be placed before him, descending gradually from the deepest to the lightest, and tis plain that he will perceive a blank, where the shade is wanting and will be sensible that there is a greater distance in that place betwixt the contiguous colours, than in any other.

And now is it not possible that they might 'raise up' to themselves, the idea of that particular shade, even 'though it had never been conveyed to them by their senses'?

The experiment appears to destroy the theory that 'simple ideas', like 'blue', are necessarily 'obtained from experience', which was indeed Hume's own view. Faced with this unpalatable possibility, Hume instead dismisses his own thought experiment as altogether too 'particular and singular' to be worth abandoning such an excellent general theory for. (We should stick to our 'colour disk illusion' instead.)

Descartes René Descartes was born in Poitiers in the last years of the sixteenth century (1596). He went to one of the first Jesuit colleges and then to university. In true Platonic fashion, he then became a soldier as a way of completing his education. Whilst in Holland with the army, he had two dreams which showed him the 'spirit of truth opening the treasures of the sciences', or the idea of applying the deductive method used, for example, in algebra to solve equations to other mathematical problems, notably geometry and, indeed, to any problems at all.

Descartes was a highly skilled mathematician, the first to discover how to describe geometric shapes with equations, using coordinate geometry – Cartesian geometry as it has become known. As far as philosophy is concerned, his most important works are the *Discourse on Method* (1637) and the *Meditations* (1641).

Descartes made the unfortunate decision, however, to accept the post of personal tutor to the Queen of Sweden, leaving his beloved Holland where he liked to spend the whole day sitting in a stone oven meditating, for freezing Sweden where the Queen liked philosophy at first light – 5 or 6 a.m. Although Socrates apparently liked to meditate in the snow, Descartes took poorly to the new lifestyle and within a year had caught a cold and died.

Descartes is considered the founder of modern philosophy, being the first philosopher since Aristotle to look at the world from first principles. Moreover, his style is fresh and original, with a conscious aim of writing for the widest possible audience – he chose to produce two versions of all his works, one in Latin, as was the norm, and one in French, for popular consumption. Until Kant reduced the subject again to esoteric monologues of professionals, philosophy became part of the living society.

Einstein Albert Einstein (1879–1955) is not generally thought of as a philosopher. But that is what he was. Einstein conducted thought experiments, which mere scientists spent much of the following sixty years testing in elaborate (and usually highly expensive) mechanical experiments. He is usually thought of as saying that everything is 'relative', a comfortable view of some succour to today's political and moral relativists. In actual fact, Einstein was interested in what was not relative, in what was absolute and unvarying, throughout the universe and throughout time. He even considered calling his theories of Special and General Relativity, 'Invariance Theory' instead.

Einstein makes absolute the speed of light, and indeed all electromagnetic energy, such as radio waves or X-rays. In order to make this possible, he had to sacrifice absolute time, and absolute space, creating instead 'space-time' (which is affected by gravity and acceleration – relative motion). But he was by no means the first to do this. The interrelationship of space and time had been discussed in strikingly similar terms by the ancient Greeks and philosophers in the intervening centuries. St Augustine thought time was dependent on there being 'observers', and Göttfried Leibniz specifically rejected the idea of absolute space or time as it would create problems regarding the origin of the universe.

Euclid invented not so much geometry, but a mathematical system for proving claims. As such, he is responsible for a lot of suffering in school classrooms.

Euclid's axioms, based on Egyptian theories, offered just five necessary assumptions upon which a pretty good geometry could be built.

They were:

> Things which are equal to the same thing are equal to one another
> If equals are added to equals the wholes are equal
> If equals are subtracted from equals, the remainders are equal
> Things which coincide with one another are equal to one another
> The whole is greater than the part

If you don't understand these, you won't like the proofs either. Euclid's approach, however, of setting out his assumptions, then proving something, and then using the 'proved thing' to further develop new proofs, citing only the number of the proof, was attractive to many subsequent philosophers, notably Spinoza and Wittgenstein.

Glossary

Frege Göttlob Frege (1848–1925) asked how numbers such as $\sqrt{-1}$, or even zero, can be related to the number of biscuits in the cookie jar, concluding that numbers referred to concepts, not things. Frege then, like Russell slightly later, tried to found mathematics on an entirely logical base, developing a new notation in the process which hardly anyone could understand, which was considered a splendid achievement. Frege took his number trick further by applying it to nouns and sentences as a whole. He discerned two types of meaning: sense, in German, *Sinn*; and reference, *Bedeutung*. (The philosophical evergreen example is of the 'Morning Star' and 'Evening Star'. Both refer to the planet Venus, which originally was thought to be two different stars, but the 'sense' of the two terms is different.) *Sinn* is essentially the 'meaning' of the word or sentence, whilst *Bedeutung* is what is being referred to (as well as being German for . . . meaning).

German language philosophy German language philosophy texts have always been rather odd – mystical even. The novice philosopher will happily plunge into Plato, Aristotle and any old English philosophers, and then enjoy reading some French and Dutch ones. Non-specialists will find Chinese, Indian and African philosophy strange, but ultimately accessible. But German philosophy – Hegel, Kant, Husserl? The books are as mentally opaque and impenetrable as they are physically thick and dense.

In 1781 the poor translator of the original English edition of Kant's great work, the *Critique of Pure Reason*, wrote in a special apologetic preface:

> He [Kant] had never studied the art of expression. He wearies by frequent repetitions, and employs a great number of words to express, in the clumsiest way, what could have been enounced more clearly and distinctly in a few.

Hear, hear to that! But this translator is not done. He continues on a more technical note, wasting words left and right for several pages, before finally concluding:

> The main statement in his sentences is often overloaded with a multitude of qualifying and explanatory clauses; and the reader is lost in a maze, from which he has great difficulty extricating himself.

At least the first works of German language philosophy, by Hildegaard of Bingen (1098–1179) and Meister Eckhart (1260–1337), for example, were straightforwardly nutty, *doof*, propelled by a serious-minded concern to explain visions of truth to the uninitiated, a task shared of course by all serious philosophers. But as well as being mystical, German language philosophy has a reputation for being heavyweight, learned – and dull. Perhaps the language itself determines this? After all, Hegel believed the variety of abstract terms available in German to far exceed any other language, whilst that old nasty, Martin Heidegger, claimed that in order to philosophise the French had to use German, as it had, he said, some excellent affinity to ancient Greek.

Whether or not this is true (which seems unlikely), Leibniz considered that the German language had both exceptional sensual and metaphorical power – and he chose to write in French or Latin instead.

Hume David Hume's (1711–76) two most celebrated works, *The Treatise on Human Nature* and *An Enquiry Concerning Human Understanding*, were, like Berkeley's writings, published before he was thirty. In 1744 he made an unsuccessful attempt to become a university professor, and on failing to achieve this became first tutor to a lunatic and then secretary to a general.

Hume applied logic to philosophy, and ended up finding no use for either. The first victim of his approach was 'consciousness', or 'the self', as an entity. He observed that consciousness is always of something, of an impression of some sort, being hot, cold or whatever, and so the self is a bundle of perceptions. No one can perceive 'the self' as such, certainly not in anyone else. Hume, thus, went one step further than Berkeley, who had demonstrated that there was no matter, by proving that there was no mind either.

Hume then examined the notion of cause and effect, which Descartes had been so keen to systematise and make certain, and decided it could yield only probable knowledge. When we see one event constantly followed by another, we 'infer' that the second event has been caused by the first. However, 'we cannot penetrate into the reason of the conjunction'. For instance, if we eat apples, we expect them to taste a certain way. If we take a bite and the apple tastes, say, of banana, we would consider it anomalous. Hume says that this is sloppy thinking. It is, in fact, another aspect of the problem of induction. 'The supposition that the future resembles the past is not founded on arguments of any kind, but is derived entirely from habit.'

From that we might conclude that all knowledge is flawed, and that we can believe nothing. Hume sees this but, in the manner of the gentleman philosopher he was, suggests that 'carelessness and inattention' offer a remedy – we should neglect the flaws in our arguments and continue to use reason whenever we find it suits us. Philosophy remains then only as an agreeable way to pass the time (he found, anyway), not a reason to change your views.

Kant Immanuel Kant (1724–1804) is often considered to have been the greatest of modern philosophers, which must say something about the rest of them. He was certainly one of the first to be actually paid for their trouble, as an academic – although he none the less continued the tradition of the early philosophers by splitting his time between lecturing on science, theoretical philosophy and even, in his case, physical geography. But unlike polymaths such as Descartes and Adam Smith, his views on science are not impressive, for example, his theory that all the planets in the solar system had intelligent life on them, with the intelligence of the life increasing the further you went from the sun, was neither very scientific nor very philosophical.

Kant's most celebrated work, which (still on the astronomical theme) he claimed as the 'Copernican revolution of philosophy', was the *Critique of Pure Reason*, published in 1781. According to Kant (with his scientific hat on), the outer world exists, but (with his philosopher one on) we can never know 'things in themselves'

Glossary

directly, only our sensations. Things-in-themselves are not part of space and time, nor are they substances, so they cannot be described with any of the normal concepts, or 'Categories' as Kant calls them. This is because space and time and all the rest are subjective, and part of our apparatus of perception. Metaphorically, they are just the spectacles through which we perceive reality. Since we always wear spatial spectacles, we always see everything in spatial terms.

One advantage of this unknowability and subjectivity for 'the-world-in-itself' is that it explains all those apparently contradictory things in life and the universe (things which Kant unhelpfully christens 'the synthetic *a priori*'), problems to do with the possibility or impossibility of free will or the question of what the universe itself is 'in' (see Problem 28), and problems pithily described by Kant in some of his celebrated 'antinomies'. Since none of our physical laws can apply to 'the-world-in-itself', free will is possible for human beings, at least, as it were, in principle (since we can have no knowledge about it one way or the other).

In *The Groundwork to the Metaphysic of Morals* (1785), Kant says we should follow the Categorical Imperative, which is to:

Glossary

> Act only according to a maxim by which you can at the same time will that it shall become a universal law.

Kant illustrates this Imperative with a few examples. One is of the act of borrowing money, without intending to pay it back on time. If everyone did this, Kant argues, then no one would trust anyone else, and the institution of promising would collapse. Being 'illogical' is what we really mean by saying something is 'wrong'. Any attempt to introduce some consideration of the effects of actions, Kant was wholly opposed to. For him, the rightness of an action depended not on its results, but only on the principle which justified it. Theft, murder and being unhelpful to others are likewise ruled out as 'illogical' and self-contradictory. This last, the 'everyone looks after number one' philosophy of living, Kant concedes is, strictly speaking, universalisable, but he maintains it still involves a contradiction as everyone at some time or other needs help.

Knowledge There are many different ways of knowing something – you can know a fact, know a friend, and you can know how to tie your shoelace. Philosophers are inclined to narrow down the task of defining knowledge to just the first, and to restrict this to tautologies. Descartes distinguished 'clear and distinct' beliefs from other ones, and called these knowledge. The Oxford linguistic philosopher J. L. Austin suggested that to say you know something is to give your word that it is so, to make a special kind of promise. (See also Problem 2.)

Locke John Locke was born in Somerset in 1632, shortly before the outbreak of the Civil War in England, and combined medicine, political service and philosophy as a career. He is generally credited with being the philosophical father of the American Constitution.

Locke is also usually accepted as the founder of 'English empiricism', although both Bacon and Hobbes had also insisted on the central role of sense experience in the search for knowledge. Locke's position is that all 'the materials of human knowledge' are gathered either directly from the physical world, through our senses or indirectly from our internal, mental world through introspection. Locke puts it this way:

> All those sublime thoughts which tower above the clouds, and reach as high as heaven itself, take their rise and footing here; in all that great extent wherein the mind wanders in those remote speculations it may seem to be elevated with, it stirs not one jot beyond those ideas which sense or reflection have offered for its contemplation.

Locke's ideas have been influential. For example, Locke distinguished between primary and secondary qualities. The primary qualities are somehow fundamental and inseparable from the object, being solidity, extension, figure, whether it is at rest or in motion, and number. The secondary qualities, on the other hand, colours, smells, sounds and so on, are 'in truth' as Locke puts it in Book II of his *Essay Concerning Human Understanding*, nothing in the objects themselves, but merely 'powers to produce various sensations in us'. A secondary quality of fire, for example, is that it produces pain. (Under certain circumstances; it may be warmth under others.) Pain is not an essential part of fire, nor is (wait for it) white an essential part of being snow.

Secondary qualities are prone to error, due to blue spectacles, a cold or whatever. But as Bishop George Berkeley pointed out, the same can be said of the primary qualities. Locke's view that the physical word consists only of matter in motion became the accepted basis of theories of sound, heat, light and electricity, and even today, when quantum mechanics works on completely different principles, much of people's understanding works on this basis, wrong or not.

In this, Locke would have no trouble. He writes of reason, in a rebuff to the suggestion that reasoning is by a logical process of syllogistic deductions: 'God has not been so sparing to men to make them barely two-legged creatures, and left it to Aristotle to make them rational.'

Logic Some philosophers will tell you that logic is advanced philosophy, perhaps even 'too difficult' for them to explain to you. Don't you believe them – it is nothing of the sort. It is since Euclid, whose elegant mathematical proofs seemed so much better than ordinary language discussions, that philosophers have been attracted towards logic – the attempt to impose order on our concepts, language and ideas. Logic is a mathematical way of looking at the world, which bears only a rather flimsy resemblance to it, entirely based on the assumptions you start with. There is a wealth of empirical – let alone intuitive – evidence that notions of reasoning as a kind of mental logic are 'false', and that instead people reason by using mental models and imagination.

None the less, much philosophical logic proceeds on the basis of Aristotle's Rules of Reasoning, which state that there are some 256 different possible types of argument of which only a few, given that they start off with true assumptions, will always produce true conclusions. Leibniz thought that logic would enable humankind to construct a machine to solve all its problems ('come, let us calculate'), a delusion all the more popular since the invention of the computer.

Logic, however, has its disadvantages. One is that it only ever produces tautologies. If you want to find out something new, you can't use it – at best it may be able to help you identify something true out of something very confused. And using it can be dangerous. As G. K. Chesterton pointed out in *Orthodoxy* (1908), it can send quite normal people into a twilight world of their own.

> Poets do not go mad; but chess players do. Mathematicians go mad, and cashiers; but creative artists very seldom. I am not, as will be seen, in any sense attacking logic: I only say that this danger does lie in logic, not in imagination.

Formal logic: Formal logic is essentially the 'science of deductive proof'. It, and the following discussion of modern logic, is included here only to indicate what it was philosophers like Frege and Russell were fiddling around with when Problem 1 so upset them. (And to warn readers not to be impressed by those who would try to confound them with unintelligible formal arguments!) The attraction of formal logic is that if the assumptions are correct, the conclusion is too, which looks useful. However, it is actually easier to see the meaningful content of real arguments when abstract symbols are replaced with meaningful content. Lewis Carroll, who as well as writing *Alice in Wonderland* was a skilled mathematician, mimicked the logicians with his 'lobster argument', which runs:

> ALL red boiled lobsters are dead
> AND all dead red lobsters are boiled
> SO all boiled dead lobsters are red.

(It doesn't tell you anything, particularly as it isn't even, in logicians' terms, deductively valid, which is his point. Try drawing a [Venn] diagram to see which bits belong where, if you're not convinced.)

Thanks, but I think maybe . . .

Glossary

Formal logic starts with Aristotle's work in the 'Prior Analytics' concerning syllogisms (an argument with two premises followed by a conclusion; in medieval times they were all given names like 'Barbara'). An example of one is:

> All apples grow on trees
> All Golden Delicious are apples
> All Golden Delicious grow on trees.

The process of inference is an 'argument', and arguments are either valid or invalid, depending upon whether they follow the rules of reasoning. This is not the same as being 'true' or 'false', which is a matter of facts, to be decided upon after investigating the actual assumptions or premises. All that is necessary for an argument to be valid is that it must follow the rules of logic, which to some extent are also the rules of reasoning, such as the Law of Non-Contradiction and the Law of Excluded Middle.

Aristotle defined four types of 'claim':

> All S are P
> No S is P
> Some S is P

Some S is not P.

These can be arranged in various ways in the syllogism, leading altogether to the 256 different possible syllogistic arguments. The great majority are invalid, and Aristotle concentrates on the valid forms. But how does he prove that the valid forms are valid? After all, the idea is to show that arguments are valid because they are one of the valid forms. It does not seem to be possible to apply this to the argument form itself. However, Aristotle argues that there are indemonstrable starting-points to any chain of reasoning. The notion of being 'self-evident' is central to his approach, but the question always lurks: 'self-evident to whom?' In any case, 'self-evident' is a psychological statement not a logical one.

A different kind of objection to his logic is that Aristotle assumed that the subject of a premise, as in 'all cats have whiskers', existed. Later logicians have wanted to avoid this, and have changed the sense to:

For any x, if that x is a cat, then that x has whiskers.

This in itself produces a gap between ordinary language and logic.

Out of all the forms a *logical* argument can take, the most celebrated are ones such as:

If I study philosophy then I become dull
I have studied philosophy
I have become dull

which is known as *modus ponens*, and is an example of a valid argument. However, the argument in the form:

If I study philosophy then I will become dull
I am dull
I have studied philosophy

is not valid.* It is a fallacy, and is so frequently found that it has a special name:

* I may be dull for another reason.

207

The Fallacy of Affirming the Consequent. (In an 'If . . . then' statement, the first part is the antecedent, and the second part is the consequent.)

One of the other main forms that a valid argument takes is known as *modus tollens*. In our example, it would be:

> If I study philosophy then I will become dull
> I am not dull
> I have not studied philosophy.

Modern logic: Modern logic is often taken as having begun in 1879, credited to Göttlob Frege (1846–1925) with additional work by Bertrand Russell (1872–1970) in the twentieth century. Where Aristotle was interested in the structure of sentences, i.e. within sentences, much of modern logic tries to treat sentences as propositions and units which are then manipulated, usually via symbols and notation.

The main ones required are:

AND	CONJUNCTION	•
OR	DISJUNCTION	∨
NOT	NEGATION	~
IF ... THEN	CONDITIONAL	–>
IFF	BI-CONDITIONAL	⇔

(Or all sorts of other funny symbols depending on the philosophers' fancies. The small print: the 'or' in logic is 'inclusive' – both possibilities are allowed to be true. If you tell a logician that you would like orange juice OR tea, don't be surprised to get an unappetising mixture. And the conditional does not imply any sort of relationship, causal or otherwise . . .)

The question to what extent logic really is the way we reason is at the heart of much of contemporary Western philosophy. For example, the definition of validity used in a standard 'formal logic' is that it must not be possible for the premises of an argument to be true and yet the conclusion to be false.

Two strange and slightly ridiculous consequences have to be swallowed even with this fairly modest assumption (see Problem 100). The first is that any argument with inconsistent premises is valid, irrespective of what the conclusions of that

Glossary

argument are. For example, if snow is always white is the first premise, and the second is that snow is sometimes not white, it follows logically that the moon is a balloon, because anything at all follows from inconsistent premises.

The other is that if a conclusion is necessarily true, then the argument is valid irrespective of what the premises were. This is because there are no circumstances in which the conclusion can be false, and the premises true, because the conclusion itself cannot be false.

Likewise, if cats can fly, then dogs can drive cars, is a perfectly valid inference, as a false statement implies any statement whatsoever. (Because the only way 'If P then Q' can be falsified is by finding a situation where P is true and Q is false, which cannot ever happen here.)

Logical Positivism In 1922, Moritz Schlick, a philosopher-scientist who had made something of a name for himself translating Einstein's theories into philosowaffle, was made Professor of Philosophy at the University of Vienna. Around Schlick formed the so-called Vienna Circle, of very dry, very scientific philosophers, who described themselves as 'Logical Positivists'. The Circle would only admit those who agreed that nothing anyone says has any meaning unless it can be checked up on using scientific procedures of 'verification'. Philosophers, of course, are still left very important, as they can check that the verified claims and indeed the unverified ones are expressed nice and logically.

If the Logical Positivists had come along a bit later, they might have liked to wear badges with the number '451' on them, after the firemen in Ray Bradbury's science-fiction thriller, *Fahrenheit 451*, whose public duty it was to go around burning the wrong sort of books. This would have been at least some small recognition of their ideological debt to the dour Scottish philosopher, David Hume (see Problem 100).

Metaphysics Originally, 'metaphysics' was just the chapter *after* or beyond 'physics' in Aristotle's philosophy. It can be defined as 'beyond science', or even 'before science', depending on taste. Or it can be defined the way H. L. Mencken (1880–1956) did in his *Notebooks: Minority Report*, as a way of increasing 'the capacity of human beings to bore one another', along, Mencken suggests, with the dinner party of more than two, and the epic poem. The Logical Positivists also had it in their sights, preferring their own brand of logico-mathematical mumbo-jumbo.

Nietzsche Friedrich Nietzsche, the nineteenth-century German philosopher favoured by Hitler, as discussed in Problem 101, was born in the Prussian town of Röcken in the 'Year of Revolutions' (1844). He first read Schopenhauer's *The World as Will and Representation* as a revelation, which he adapted to his own, rather dubious, ends. Nietzsche saw human beings, and indeed all life, as engaged in a struggle to increase their *power*.

Nietzsche was a philosopher-poet who wrote of 'Supermen' and battles, yet Nietzsche, the historical man, was prone to ill-health, headaches and chronic short sight, along with intestinal problems, cutting, in many ways, a tragic figure. At one point, Nietzsche blames, rather feebly, the weather for making him a 'narrow, withdrawn, grumpy specialist' instead of a significant, brave 'spirit'.Then again, he says that his sickness 'liberated me slowly', by forcing him to give up his teaching and books, and instead to break his habits, and above all, to 'put an end to all bookwormishness'.

Nietzsche's intention, as we have already seen in the discussion of Problem 101, in declaring himself the 'first immoralist', was to 'revalue' all values, starting with the unmasking of Christianity and literally making 'good' 'bad', but this task was never completed. Instead *Ecce Homo*, 'Behold the Man', has to stand as his definitive work, for early in 1889 he descended into madness.

Again, Nietzsche wrote too that the goal of humanity is not in some supposed general strategy or process, such as the maximisation of happiness, but is to be found in the activities of its 'highest specimens'. 'The man who would not belong in the mass needs only to cease being comfortable with himself; he should follow his conscience which shouts at him: "Be yourself!" You are not really all you do, think, and desire now.' His discussion of the 'master/slave' relationship in *The Will to Power*, where he explains all behaviour as power-seeking, is the most telling. The 'Superman', or *Übermensch*, is for Nietzsche the logical outcome of his theory, an individual enjoying his power to the full, untrammelled by notions of justice or pity.

In the concluding chapter to *Ecce Homo*, 'Why I Am Destiny', Nietzsche writes:

> I know my fate. One day, there will be associated with my name the recollection of something frightful – of a crisis like no other before on earth, of the profoundest collision of conscience, of a decision evoked against

everything that until then had been believed in, demanded, sanctified. I am not a man, I am dynamite.

Nietzsche's writings are not really terribly good literature – but the philosophers think they are. And they are not really terribly good philosophy – but the literary critics think they are. In this way, he has been able to retain a largely undeserved reputation for profundity and originality.

Oriental Philosophy Eastern philosophy is holistic. The Eastern philosophers don't like to divide everything up like the Western 'analytic' philosophers in the tradition of Aristotle (who suffered from a particularly severe taxonomical disorder). But, in fact, there is quite a lot of Eastern philosophy in Western philosophy, starting with Plato, who stressed the importance of 'balance' and 'harmony', two Eastern concepts. Plato also reflects the oriental emphasis on philosophy as both theory: learning and knowing, and practice: living and being.

Chinese philosophies, in particular, regard thinking and acting as two aspects of one activity – two sides of the same coin. *T'ai Chi* – ultimate reality – is a combination of mind (*li*) and matter (*chi*).The aim is to align yourself with the *Tao*. But what is the *Tao*?

Tao is empty. Lao Tzu wrote in the fourth chapter of the *Tao Te Ching* a description of *Tao* that might also, equally well, serve as a description of philosophy:

> like a bowl, it may be used, but is never emptied, it is bottomless, the ancestor of all things, it blunts sharpness, it unties knots, it softens the light, it becomes one with the dusty world – deep and still, it exists for ever.

(See also **The Upanishads**; the discussions of Problems 79–90.)

Plato Plato was born in 427 BC into a distinguished Athenian family with political connections, particularly with the democratic and oligarchic movements. He himself had political ambitions, and his book *The Republic*, written in the form of a little playlet, starring Socrates, is not only a blueprint of all subsequent Western philosophical thought, but also a political manifesto. The first aim, however, has proved to be the more lasting. Plato introduced the distinction between mind and matter, highlighted later by Descartes, and he also produced a strange theory of heavenly ideas, or forms, one of which existed for every concept we have. There was a heavenly form of beauty and truth, of course, but also one of 'threeness' or 'fourness', 'chairness' – even 'ugliness' – although Plato didn't like to talk about this much.

Russell Bertrand Arthur William Russell (1872–1970), Third Earl, grandson of a Victorian prime minister, was a peculiar mixture of logical mathematician and radical free-thinker. His life was divided between unsuccessful efforts to find a secure logical base for mathematics, notably in his *Principia Mathematica* (1910–13), his popular philosophy, notably the aforementioned *Problems of Philosophy* and the door-stopping *History of Western Philosophy* – not to mention time spent in prison. This indignity came in 1918 when his principled opposition to the pointless slaughter that was the First World War led to prosecution as a pacifist.

In his philosophy, as already noted, he failed to solve any of the key problems – but had a jolly good try. Similarly, his distinction between two types of knowledge, what the French call *savoir* and *connaître* – and what he called knowledge by acquaintance or by description (or *vice versa*), the former kind being the more immediate and certain – has not been treated too kindly by posterity either. However, he did receive a consolation Nobel Prize in 1950 – for literature.

St Augustine Aurelius Augustinius was born in 355 in the area we now know as Algeria, and studied in North Africa, finishing eventually at Carthage, the capital of Roman Africa. His education was primarily literary and rhetorical, and he became Professor of Rhetoric in due course at both Carthage and Milan. However, he soon abandoned his successful career as an academic to follow the promptings of his religious conscience. He managed to combine his writing with this, however, and produced a substantial body of works, notably scriptural commentaries, doctrinal debates, historical works on the influence of paganism and, most influentially, the *Confessions*, an account of his own spiritual awakening.

Typical of these confessions is the seven-chapter description of the self-torment occasioned by the childhood folly when he robbed a neighbour's pear tree, without even being hungry. It was, he realised later, an act of pure mischief – or wickedness.

> Behold my heart, O God, behold my heart, which Thou hadst pity upon in the bottom of the abyss. Now, behold, let my heart tell Thee, what it sought there, that I should be gratuitously wicked, having no temptation to that evil deed, but the evil deed itself. It was foul, and I loved it; I loved to perish, I loved mine

own fault, not that of the sake of which I committed the fault, but my fault itself I loved.

The other major source of personal self-hatred for Augustine was lust. He considered sexual intercourse to be a necessary physical act, like making a table, but its accompaniment by sexual passion, and general irrationality, made it a wicked sin. The saint himself had, in addition to a wife, several mistresses but he was clear in his own mind what the proper course was, writing famously: 'Give me chastity and continence, only not yet.'

(See also the discussions of Problems 81–90 and 96–97.)

(Not to be confused with: *Saint Anselm*.)

It was Anselm who devised one of the most ambitious arguments for the existence of God – namely that it was logically impossible for God not to. The so-called 'ontological' argument was succinctly characterised by C. S. Lewis in his poem on Descartes, 'Abecedarium Philosophicum':

D for Descartes who said 'God couldn't be
So complete if he weren't.'
So he is,
Q.E.D.

Sartre Jean-Paul Sartre (1905–80) is that rare creature – a philosopher who can write. Albeit, he never managed to combine the two skills. Although he wrote a number of very exciting books such as *Nausea* resulting, presumably, from his philosophical works, such as *Being and Nothingness* and *Existentialism and Humanism*, the philosophical works are quite phenomenologically dull, littered with dead and dying words like a wood after a hurricane.

In general, Sartre reflects a blend of influences. From the likes of Martin Heidegger and Friedrich Nietzsche come intolerance of 'bourgeois morality' and his celebrated description of other people as a kind of 'hell'. Then, from the progressive socialist aspirations of Paris generally and feminists in particular, such as Simone de Beauvoir, prime amongst many Sartrean dalliances, comes a much more humanist concern.

Schopenhauer Arthur Schopenhauer (so-called to facilitate a career in business as 'Arthur' is a name in several European languages) was born in 1788 and died in 1860. Sent to boarding school in Wimbledon around the age of sixteen, he developed rather a lonely streak, as noted in Problems 96 and 97, observing that 'company was a fire at which man warms himself at a distance'. Originally, Schopenhauer studied medicine, but ended up with philosophy, in particular, Plato, Kant and the ancient Hindu philosophy of the *Upanishads*. Together these were the three ingredients of Schopenhauer's proto-existentialist (for want of a better word) work: *The World as Will and Representation*.

Schopenhauer's main idea, developed early, was that beyond the everyday world of experience is a better world in which the human mind pierces appearance to perceive reality. There is *Vorstellung* (representation) and *Wille* (will), which is, he argues, what the world is, in itself.

Schopenhauer makes sex the centrepiece of his philosophy, noting iconoclastically that it is the central concern of individuals, rather than the more reputable 'problems of philosophy'. He wrote (as noted earlier) that 'the genitals are the focus of the will', and says that love is the expression of the species' need to reproduce. It ebbs away as soon as the genetic function has been fulfilled. However, he, like Plato, or Buddhists, feels that there is a path on which it is possible to transcend this *Wille* and simply 'contemplate reality without striving and pain'.

Schopenhauer was a contemporary of Hegel, but was wholly opposed to him. Invited to lecture in Berlin in 1820, he chose to speak at the same time as the then professor of philosophy at the peak of his career. He resented the small audience that attended his talk, and he resolved never to lecture again. 'The emblem at the head of Hegelian university philosophy', he wrote pithily, should be a 'cuttlefish creating a cloud of obscurity around itself so that no one sees what it is, with the legend, *mea caligne tutus* [fortified by my own obscurity].' (The cuttlefish squirts out puffs of ink when threatened.)

Socrates Socrates' (fifth century BC) position in European thought is akin to that of a religious leader who, although he himself wrote nothing, has had tremendous influence through the accounts of his followers, of whom Plato is only the most notable. The style of *The Republic* is also religious in tone, with Socrates in effect extolling the need to come to know 'the Good', which some commentators see as indistinguishable from 'God', and certainly has many similarities.

In his later years, when Plato knew him, Socrates devoted himself to the discussion of ethical questions. The Oracle at Delphi, in response to an enquiry by one of his admirers, reputedly said that Socrates was the wisest man in all Greece. Socrates was sure that this could not be so, as he knew that really he knew nothing, and resolved to prove the Oracle wrong. He therefore set out by cross-questioning others to find someone who at least knew something. In practice, this revolved around exploring knowledge of ethical matters, as the Greeks equated wisdom very closely with ethical understanding. Socrates found that people either did not know, or at least could not explain, what they believed to be the case with questions on the true nature of justice, beauty, triangularity, etc. Inasmuch as Socrates *knew* he did not know, the Oracle was thus shown to be right to say that he was the wiser.

Of course, Socrates' cross-examinations were not necessarily popular, nor was his iconoclasm, whether merely implied or overt. Socrates was linked in many Athenian minds with scepticism, which was felt to be 'modern nonsense', at least partly to blame for the disasters of the war. Whatever the immediate cause of Socrates' trial or the details of his indictment, it was this, classicists believe, that led his fellow countrymen to condemn him to death.

In a letter written from prison, Plato has Socrates say:

> I came to the conclusion that all existing states were badly governed, and that their constitutions were incapable of reform without drastic treatment and a great deal of good luck. I was forced, in fact, to the belief that the only hope of finding justice for society or for the individual lay in true philosophy, and that mankind will have no respite from trouble until either real philosophers gain political power or politicians become by some miracle true philosophers.

Space 'Philosophy of Space' is a neglected area of study in philosophy departments these days. After all, Kant, along with one of his complicated theories about the *a priori*, made rather a hostage of himself with his theory that there was intelligent life on all the planets with the intelligence increasing the further out from the sun you went. (And most of the others had their cosmic hobby horses.) But, fortunately for scientific progress, it was not always so. As mentioned in the discussion of Problem 28, Democritus said simply the void was what 'was not', Aristotle that it was only a feature to be inferred from the presence of real objects,

215

and Descartes, contrariwise, that Space itself was a real object, a form of matter without any of the usual attributes such as being solid, or anything really. . . . Plato, who has the definitive word on this, as on so many other matters, thought that Space was a very special kind of thing neither made of matter like the rest of the universe, nor yet entirely abstract, like the 'Forms' themselves. It was something in between.

Socrates' friend, Timaeus, explains in the dialogue of the same name that it is: 'An invisible and characterless thing, that receives all things and shares in a perplexing way all that is intelligible'. The only way to investigate its properties is by 'a kind of groundless [i.e. no rational base] reasoning that does not involve sense perception'. (For example, as in a dreamlike trance.)

This is more sophisticated than most other philosophers and indeed physicists up to and perhaps including Einstein. (But not the latest batch of 'sub-atomic' theorists.) Certainly, Descartes and the bumbling Kant insisted that pure reason alone was enough to tell us about Space, whilst most of the rest, following Aristotle and Newton, even thought that Space was amenable to empirical and experimental investigation, and ended up with a highly theoretical 'Absolute Space' which didn't even fit the facts.

And Plato's approach has elements of relativity in it. When objects are 'impressed' onto the flux, it in turn changes, and, in changing, affects the objects again, 'it sways irregularly in every direction as it is shaken by those things, and being set in motion it in turn shakes them'. Matter acts on Space and Space acts on matter. This is pretty well Einstein's Theory of Relativity in a nutshell, and there's more than 2,000 years in between.

Spanish Philosophy Why should Spanish-speaking philosophers want to read *101 Philosophy Problems*? Apart from the surrealist excellence of the paradoxical pictures, of course. . . Or perhaps they might be refugees from the theories of José Ortega y Gasset – who developed the theory of *ratiovitalism* to counteract the 'problem of Spanish decadence'.

But although this book has little explicit reference to the Spanish philosophical tradition, there are many areas of common purpose. Which is not surprising, as Western philosophy is drawn largely from the Greeks, mediated through the Toledo 'School of Translators' during the Middle Ages. Spain is the key link in the chain between ancient Greece and the rest of Europe.

And where the Spanish mystics produced long prose poems offering love as the way (to God), and philosophers such as J. L. Vives announced the vital importance of subjectivity, the English, in particular, set their grey, cold, pinched faces against it, and proclaimed instead the centrality of 'analysis' and importance of detachment.

Spanish philosophy today is representative of a general rebellion against a certain type of Anglo-American philosophy, and a return to an older and more inclusive European tradition. After all, as Father Sanchez (1530–1623) proclaimed, distrusting philosophical authority and tradition as foundations for knowledge, 'nothing is known'. Presumably, this is not as an invitation to empty relativism, but in the manner of doubting René Descartes.

Spinoza Einstein's favourite philosopher. Dutch spectacle maker who turned down a chair in philosophy at Heidelberg to continue his polishing and grinding. Benedict Spinoza (1632–77) thought that everything was one thing – mind and body were two aspects of something else, which has many aspects including that of being God. The gist of his writings is nearer the Eastern than the Western tradition, although their style, heavily footnoted and pettifogging, is very much a product of the West.

Structuralism Structuralism originated with the linguistic philosophy of Ferdinand de Saussure (1857–1913) whose work became trendy in the second half of the twentieth century. Saussure's idea was that it is the structure of language, rather than the rules of logic, that explains how we think and speak. His notion of the 'sign' and of language as a system, called semiology, resurrected an older distinction between the structure of language, which he now called *langue*, and manifestations of *langue*, called *parole*. Chess can be used to illustrate this. The rules exist only in abstract, but their embodiment is a particular game. Language is a system of signs used to express ideas – comparable to writing, to sign-language for deaf people, and to symbolic rituals. The sign, of course, is arbitrary. It is only the system that gives signs their meaning.

Claude Lévi-Strauss rediscovered this structural linguistics and applied it to culture as a whole, as an anthropologist. He believed that since language was humanity's distinctive feature, it also defined cultural phenomena. If you speak of humanity you speak of language, and if you speak of language you speak of society. Structuralists looked below the surface of words to discover the hidden signifying system – the *langue*. All philosophical problems became problems of analysing systems of signs that structured the world. In this respect, the structuralists are harking back to the ancient Chinese 'School of Names' (*c*.380 BC), a group of early logicians with an equally theoretical interest in the relationship of language and reality.

The structuralists offer an explanation of sorts for some of the paradoxes mentioned in this book: what we know about the external world we apprehend through our senses. The phenomena which we perceive have the characteristics which we attribute to them because of the way our senses operate and the way the human brain is designed to order and interpret the stimuli which are fed into it. One very important feature of this ordering process is that we cut up the continua of space and time with which we are surrounded into segments, so that we are predisposed to think of the environment as consisting of vast numbers of separate things belonging to named classes, and to think of the passage of time as consisting of sequences of separate events.

What had started as a theoretical method for understanding language became an all embracing philosophy. Everything, even the unconscious mind, was said to be structured like a language. Everything became predetermined and fixed. Later, Michel Foucault developed a theory that power operates through complex social structures, which incorporated the view that far from knowledge and truth being fixed, they were constantly changing. He was in some respects the first post-structuralist.

Jacques Derrida attempted to pull down the structuralist edifice when he wrote that their creations were merely metaphysical imaginings. To look for a science of signs was as irrelevant, he said, as Descartes' suggestion that the body and soul ran together like two synchronised clocks. The way concepts have been used historically, and philosophy's claims to grapple with truth, are a pretence. The whole exercise was nothing but jiggery pokery – the ancient nomadic term for doing things with words.

Tautologies Tautologies are the saying of the same thing twice, only in different words. Sentences such as 'The fair will be held on either Saturday or Sunday, or at the weekend', are tautologies, but so also are apparently meaningful ones such as 'snow is frozen water' or even the famous '2 + 2 = 4'. They are attractive to philosophers because they look pretty likely to be true. The ancient Greeks particularly liked geometrical truths, such as the fact that the three angles of a triangle will add up to 180°, or that the square on the hypotenuse is equal to the sum of the squares on the other two sides.

A lot of scientific 'knowledge' can be said to be tautologous – water boils at 100° and 100 degrees centigrade is defined as the temperature that water boils at, whilst each molecule is made up of two hydrogen atoms and one oxygen atom. (Leading to one of the traditional philosophy problems seen earlier.) Wittgenstein identified tautologies as being particularly important for logic – in fact, he wrote that all truth in logic was tautology. His preferred example was that it is either raining or not raining, a peculiarly problematic example, but then Wittgenstein was a peculiar Austrian maths teacher (see below).

Logic says things like:

> If we always have either strawberry jam or raspberry jam for tea
> And we do not have any raspberry jam today
> Then we know it is strawberry jam for tea today.

(Only in less user-friendly form.)

Mathematical and logical proofs are just ways of identifying the tautology hidden in lots of essentially irrelevant sub-clauses.

Time Plato called time 'a moving image of eternity', which although poetic, is not very helpful. Aristotle discussed the nature of 'time' in more detail in his writings on 'Physics', saying that time is an effect of change in the material world. Since objects change in a smoothly continuous way, so, he deduced, must time be a continuum. Of course, as Plotinus pointed out shortly after, this definition of time involves reference to the thing being discussed, the mark of a bad definition. Plotinus himself moved beyond the physical world to make time a feature of the soul passing from one stage to another. We could also reinterpret this by saying that time is a feature of consciousness, and that without consciousness, there is no time. As Plotinus put it, 'Time is in every Soul of the order of the All-Soul, present in like form in all; for all the Souls are the one Soul'. This is why time has the character of encompassing everything, being one whole.

Be that as it may, even Plotinus' definition seems to involve time in the concept of 'passing from one stage to another', so it is not strictly speaking any better than Aristotle's.

Some philosophers have wondered about that strange quality of time whereby, in T. S. Eliot's phrase, it is a 'pattern of timeless moments'. Everything hinges on that infinitely brief moment of the present, the fountain where 'the river of time gushes out of nothingness', producing the bottomless lake of the past, and events, having 'swum into being and floated away', are eternally real, whilst the future does not exist at all. Oriental philosophy emphasises existence being poised between being and not being – yang and yin. As for our own 'being', as St Augustine pondered too, that is precariously balanced between the twin abysses of 'not yet' and 'no longer'.

Truth A problematic word in itself for philosophers. Plato said something was true if it describes things as they are, a definition which has not been improved on despite being entirely useless. William James offered as an alternative that something was true if it had useful consequences – the pragmatic theory – but even the most relativist amongst us have qualms at this approach.

Glossary

John Dewey, the American philosopher of education, wrote that 'meaning is wider in scope as well as more precious in value than truth, and philosophy is occupied with meaning rather than truth'.

Not to mention truth values – of which there are normally two, being true or false, but (see Problem 53 on ship battles) some say there is also a third, 'undetermined' truth value.

The Upanishads *The Upanishads* epic poem is a description of the unity of all existence. Indian philosophy put the emphasis on 'wisdom'. Three thousand years ago the Indian sages who influenced much of Western philosophy decided that the nature of 'ultimate reality' is that we ourselves are part of it. If we delve into ourselves we will at last find Atman, the essential self. And if we delve deeper still into the 'not-self' of external reality, we will find Brahman, which is ultimate reality. And then we will recognise that Brahman and Atman are two sides of the same.

Utilitarianism The most important ethical principle for considering the consequence of actions is that of utilitarianism, formulated by Jeremy Bentham as saying that the right action is the one that brings about the greatest happiness of the greatest number. General happiness is best. John Stuart Mill (1806–73) adopted this theory and specifically rejected alternative moral theories as representing the interests of the ruling class, not of justice. Those who taught the virtue of a life of sacrifice, Mill wrote, wanted others to sacrifice their lives to them. Mill and Bentham assume that people desire to be happy, and that this is actually the only thing they desire. When people's desires conflict, the utilitarian theory is supposed to weigh up the consequences and decide which action produces the greater happiness.

Wittgenstein Ludwig Wittgenstein was a peculiar maths teacher-soldier-engineer, and, eventually – reluctantly – philosopher. His most important contribution to philosophy was to be found in various kinds of combat. By attempting to disagree with all previous philosophers he injected a certain amount of dynamism and new vigour into debates at the start of the twentieth century. But he did not confine himself to intellectual challenges. When the First World War broke out in 1914, Wittgenstein was first on the train from Skjolden to Vienna to join the Austrian army. Serving initially on a naval boat and then in an artillery workshop, in 1916 he was lucky enough to be assigned to a howitzer regiment on the Russian front where he gained several citations for bravery. In 1918 he was promoted and sent to north Italy to serve in an artillery regiment where he still was at the end of the war, becoming a prisoner of the Allies. (It doesn't fit in very well with today's conventional picture of the academic scholar, but Plato would have been proud of him.)

Wittgenstein's combative approach had of course emerged earlier. At school, he even (to his credit) apparently fell out with a Mr A. Hitler (no seriously!); later a teaching career in schools was abandoned after much shouting at children in maths class (he was eventually persuaded to desist from teaching after an Austrian police investigation into an incident which left a child unconscious!); and throughout he tended to fall out with his family of wealthy industrialists, who propelled him with difficulty towards an engineering degree in Britain.

But once there, Wittgenstein made heavy weather of his attempts to design a plane powered by gases fired at the propellers, berating his employees in his aeronautics laboratory. His engineer relates how 'when things went wrong, which often occurred, he would throw his arms about, stamp around and swear volubly in German' (in a passage quoted by Ray Monk in his biography of Wittgenstein).

So it was with propeller design in mind that Wittgenstein arrived at Oxford to learn a bit more about the mathematics of aircraft design, and fell into a more constructive relationship with the distinguished philosopher Bertrand Russell – whom he completely disagreed with. Then there is the strange story of how, much later, in 1946, at a meeting of the Cambridge Moral Science Club, he brandished a red hot poker at Karl Popper, demanding to know what Popper meant by 'ethical rules'. When Popper said these were statements such as (for example) 'it is wrong to threaten visiting speakers with pokers', Wittgenstein stormed out.

Wittgenstein is *also* known for having written two philosophy books. The first book, in 1922, in which he numbered each sentence as he went along, in a self-conscious attempt at indicating the importance of his insights, is the *Tractatus Logico-Philosophicus*. This says that all philosophy problems have been solved, and is straightforwardly in opposition to this work.

Wittgenstein was at this time distinctly Logical Positivist in flavour, considering words to be directly linked to reality (what anthropologists call the 'Bow wow wow' theory of language), in the way that a police model of an accident resembles the accident. Where this simple notion fell down, such as it does in most of ethics, metaphysics and indeed philosophy, he followed the Logical Positivists, dismissing the talk as empty grunting and nonsense. As he puts it, twice, in the *Tractatus*: 'whereof one cannot speak, one must remain silent'.

Some say, however, that he actually thought that even if it was not possible to *say* anything about anything very much, it was possible to *show* it. In his later, posthumously published book, *Philosophical Investigations*, he reversed many of his earlier findings, and compared words and sentences to the tools in a toolbox, or to the controls of a locomotive, saying that meaning is use. If that seems hard to grasp, in his 'Miscellaneous Remarks on Culture', Wittgenstein advises that sometimes 'a sentence can be understood only if read at the right tempo. My sentences are all supposed to be read slowly.' But then, he also later acknowledges the similarity between a philosopher's use of words and a young child's use of crayons. The philosopher's, like the child's, claims of what their scribbles 'represent' should not be taken too seriously.

These days he is very highly regarded by academic philosophers, many of whom erroneously credit him with insights, such as the theory of 'family resemblances', for explaining how terms come about, that correctly belong to others.

Zeno Zeno of Elea (fifth century BC) is so old that he is older in fact than Plato and Socrates. He is even older than Euclid, whose fabulous geometrical systems, developed from those of the North Africans, so impressed the philosophers. But none the less, much of Zeno is about geometry and the nature of numbers – particularly the strange quantities, infinity and zero.

The reasoning behind Zeno's paradoxes is described, ostensibly by the man himself, in Plato's dialogue *Parmenides*. There, almost uniquely, Socrates is given a verbal pasting by Zeno over the matter of whether it makes any difference to say the universe is 'all one' or 'definitely not many'. (But Socrates was then still very young!)

Zeno is reading his book to Socrates and Parmenides. (Unfortunately, Zeno's book got lost somewhere down the millennia. However, Simplicius [sixth century AD] appeared to have a copy of it to hand when he wrote his account, and gives a much more considered version of the arguments than many commentators before [notably Aristotle] or since.)

SOCRATES: Parmenides, I understand that Zeno wants to be on intimate terms with you not only in friendship but in his book. He has, in a way, written the same thing as you, only changing it around so as to fool us into thinking he has said something different. You say in your poem that all is one, and you give splendid and elegant proofs for that; and he, for his part, that everything is 'not many', and gives a vast array of excellent proofs for that of his own. So with one of you saying 'one' and the other saying 'not many', and with each of you speaking in a way that sounds as if you are not saying the same thing – even though you mean practically the same thing – what you say seems to be said over the top of heads of the rest of us!

ZENO: Yes, Socrates, but you still haven't discerned the main point about my book, although you have chased its arguments and followed their scents with the enthusiasm of a young Spartan hound. First of all, you have missed this point: the book doesn't at all preen itself on having been written with the secret intention you describe, whilst disguising its purpose from people, as if that were some great accomplishment. You have mentioned something that happened accidentally. The truth is that the book comes to the defence of Parmenides' argument against those who say that if everything is one, it leads to absurdities and self-contradictions. Accordingly, my book pays them back in kind, with something for good measure, since it aims to show that their approach, that the universe is many, would, if someone examined the matter thoroughly, result in consequences even more absurd than those suffered by it being one. I wrote a book, then, in that competitive spirit, when I was a young man. Someone made a copy without consulting me, so I didn't even have a chance to decide whether it should see the light.

Many people are convinced that Zeno's arguments have been settled through the application of modern (read 'latest thinking') mathematics. But the Eleatics, of whom Zeno is only the most famous member, were making a more genuinely philosophical point. They wanted to show that if time is a continuous flow, then there can be no present, but if time is made up of a sequence of separate moments, then there can *only* be the present one. (And, incidentally, change is an illusion.) This is what the hare rushes to show us. On the other hand, if space is all just one, there can be no notion of 'here' or place. If space can be broken into smaller parts, then there is only here – and no motion. And that is what the 'arrow' is doing. But his problems do put it rather more elegantly!

Reading guide

Many of the problems are essentially concerned with metaphysical issues, issues lying beyond 'science', such as the nature of the universe, of time and of 'fundamental reality'. These, of course, have been of interest to a great many philosophers through the ages but, increasingly today, much of the most interesting work in these areas is done by those whom we would normally call scientists. Astronomers such as Carl Sagan and Frederick Hoyle raise many of the issues regarding the nature of the universe, and sub-atomic physics, as described so attractively and clearly by Fritjof Capra or Nigel Hawkes, increasingly resembles not just philosophy but, as Capra points out, religion. Two good books are Fritjof Capra, *The Tao of Physics* (Wildwood House, New York, 1975) and Nigel Calder, *Einstein's Universe* (Penguin, London and New York, 1979). My own collection of 'thought experiments' in science and philosophy, *Wittgenstein's Beetle and Other Classic Thought Experiments* (Blackwell, 2004) covers many of these issues too, along with a few of the slightly more juicy philosophic experiments on issues of mind and identity.

A very good 'source book' for philosophy of space and infinity and things like that is *Space from Zeno to Einstein* by Nick Huggett (MIT Press, 1999). There, readers will find all the philosophical gems, from the few remaining scraps of Zeno's theories and views to extracts from later theoretical physics. Readers will find, accompanying these extracts, clear and well-written commentaries, but should avoid the textbook-style exercises which are more likely to depress than enlighten them! I should like to acknowledge being encouraged by J. Baginni to include Problems 45 and 46, on 'personal identity' after seeing his collection of 100 philosophy problems entitled *The Pig That Wants to be Eaten and 99 Other Thought Experiments* (2005), which although it has much the same format and content as this collection of philosophy problems, he assured me has its own, entirely independent, personal identity.

The Hackett Publishing Company, Indianapolis, USA, produce probably the cheapest collection of classical philosophy texts, including those of Descartes, Plato's dialogues, John Locke's *Second Treatise on Government,* David Hume's *An Enquiry Concerning Human Understanding* and John Stuart Mill's *Utilitarianism* and

On Liberty. These combine to make a good, basic 'philosophical library' (or doorstop). Actually, an even quicker shortcut to a good philosophical library is Graham Higgin's collection of fossilised philosophical quotations, *Porcupines* (Penguin, 1999) in which he identifies a fragment or 'fossil', and reproduces it in large type capable of making even some of the most unpromising philosophical material look interesting. And another of my own books, *Philosophical Tales* (Blackwell, 2006) as well as offering a clear introduction to the great works of philosophy, also provides a rare glimpse of the 'other side' of the famous philosophers, the bits that they would rather history forgot about.

Readers interested in artificial intelligence, and who want to know how intelligent they are really (the machines, that is), might like to consult Rainer Born's collection of essays in *Artificial Intelligence: The Case Against* (Croom Helm, London, 1987). This includes John Searle's well-known discussion of the possibilities of communicating with an English-speaking-someone in another room using written Chinese – what has become known as the 'Chinese Room' problem – the idea being that this process illustrates what it is like to be a computer.

And those intrigued by the mathematical nature of some of the paradoxes might like to find 2^8 (a lot, anyway) of them, including a version of Problem 1, in *What Is The Name of This Book?* by Raymond Smullyan (Penguin, London, 1978). However, attractively presented though this work is, it is more a rather narrow sort of mathematical exercise book than a philosophical exploration (along the lines of the sort of thing that appears in puzzle columns). Chris Ormell's booklet *Some Varieties of Superparadox* (1993, obtainable from MAG-Ashby, PO Box 16916, London) is a more stimulating and profound discussion – most definitely philosophical.

Problems 11–23 and 72–78 are broadly 'ethical' ones, concerned with calculations of 'right or wrong'. The companion book to this one, *101 Ethical Dilemmas* (Routledge, 2002, 2nd edn 2007) offers many more scenarios and much more detailed discussion of ethical issues than is possible here. One of the most important questions here is whether there is, in fact, any such distinction, which some would say takes us straight back into metaphysics. But if we assume there is, then we may aspire to have a clear idea of how to set about calculating it. Peter Singer has produced a clearly and thoughtfully written account of one approach – the utilitarian one – in his book *Practical Ethics* (Cambridge University Press, Cambridge, 1979, 2nd edn 1993). But this account is not uncontroversial – some German universities banned him from speaking in them because of sensitivity at the implications of this book for, amongst others, the handicapped (he says they can be killed at birth). An alternative and profoundly humanistic account of ethics can be found in Brenda Almond's *Exploring Ethics* (Blackwell, Oxford, 1998), which also uses, like this book, the vehicle of narrative fiction to explore, as the title puts it, various theories and issues in morality.

The Lost Kingdom of Marjon was grateful, no doubt, for the work of John Rawls, whose views can be tracked down in *A Theory of Justice,* or specifically the essay 'Justice as Fairness' in *Philosophy, Politics and Society*, edited by Peter Laslett and W. G. Runciman (Blackwell, Oxford, 1962). The decision to overthrow the Community Council can be compared to other decisions to adopt direct action, one particular perspective on which is that of Martin Luther King, the American Civil Rights leader, to be found in his essay on the famous Montgomery bus boycott in *Slide Towards Freedom: the Montgomery Story* (Harper & Row, New York, 1958). My book, *Political Philosophy from Plato to Mao* (Pluto, 2001) also discusses these issues.

The medical ethics scenarios owe something to the work of Judith Jarvis Thomson, whose own essay 'In Defense of Abortion' appeared originally in the academic journal, *Philosophy and Public Affairs*, fall 1971, and has been reprinted subsequently in many books on ethics (including Singer's *Applied Ethics*).

The 'dispositional' problems raise general issues of psychology as well as of free will, punishment and the law. Some of these arguments can be seen employed controversially by the American lawyer, Clarence Darrow, in defence of child-killers and other assorted murderers. See 'Darrow, Attorney for the Damned', in the collection of essays, *Philosophy, Paradox and Discovery*, edited by Arthur Minton (McGraw-Hill, New York, 1976).

The problems of the sleeping man, and the more general issues of free will in general (Problems 52 and 53) can be traced back to the philosophies of John Locke and Benedict Spinoza (1632–77), whilst a more recent perspective, that of people being behaviourist machines, can be examined in the work of behaviourism's 'founding father', John Watson (1878–1958) or in the more accessible accounts of the arch-animal experimenter, B. F. Skinner. Watson once said that, given a dozen 'healthy infants', he could produce to specification, doctors, lawyers, artists or beggarmen and thieves. (See *Behaviourism*, Kegan Paul, London, 1925.) Since the discovery in 1953 of DNA, this attitude towards people has been reinforced.

Readers interested in ship battles may also like to see A. J. Ayer's essay 'Fatalism' in *The Concept of a Person* (Macmillan, London, 1963) where he suggests that the important thing is the difference between what will be and what must be.

The *principles* of utilitarianism, the system behind the 'hedonic calculus' used by the sleeper, the Marjonians and doubtless many hospital ethics committees too, can be examined in their original form in the writings of Jeremy Bentham and John Stuart Mill, particularly Mill's *Utilitarianism, Liberty and Representative Government*. Contemporary accounts are: *Utilitarianism: For and Against*, J. J. C. Smart and Bernard Williams (Cambridge University Press, Cambridge, 1973); *The Rational Foundation of Ethics*, Timothy Sprigge (Routledge and Kegan Paul, London, 1988). One of the best accounts of time is J. B. Priestly's *Man and Time* (Aldus, London, 1964), which includes some bizarre stories of time-defeating premonitions sent to him by correspondents.

Other Problems (31, 47 and 48) are concerned with the nature of artistic judgements, an area known to academics as aesthetics, whilst the problems of the 'Value of stamps and potatoes' are raising issues in the social sciences, an area known to philosophers as 'not philosophy' at all! None the less, both areas are historically of great concern to philosophers, for the reasons explained particularly clearly in Nigel Warburton's *Philosophy: The Basics* (Routledge, London, 1996, 2nd edn). Bertrand Russell and J. M. Keynes corresponded at length over their shared interests in the issues of probability and induction, and the reader, as always, could do worse than start with the account of economic development and aesthetics in Plato's *The Republic*. Finally, the experiments with popular elements for pictures, mentioned in the discussion of Problem 31, can be found in *Komar and Melamid's Scientific Guide to Art*, published in the USA by Farrar, Strauss and Giroux, 1998.

Books on all aspects of philosophy

Bertrand Russell's much reprinted and still unmatched *History of Western Philosophy* contains numerous short 'vignette' accounts of individual philosophers and their ideas (Routledge, London, 2000). Two good, recent books for the general reader are the amusing and clear *Philosophy: A–Z*, Nigel Warburton (Routledge, London, 1998), and the elegantly crafted *Exploring Philosophy*, Brenda Almond (Blackwell, Oxford, 1995).

The collection of scholarly but still largely well-written essays on many aspects of Western philosophy in *A Critical History of Western Philosophy*, Dan O'Connor (Macmillan, London, 1985) or, on a completely different note, the entertaining and not wholly uninformative *Philosophy for Beginners* by Richard Osborne, one of a series of 'cartoon' versions of philosophers (Writers and Readers Press, New York, 1994), may also whet some philosophical appetites.

Acknowledgements

I should like to thank the fictive Professor Highly Dull for his invaluable comments on the last paragraph of Problem 30, and my dog, Blackie, for patiently typing the whole manuscript four times. Any mistakes are Professor Dull's, and not mine. Or possibly Blackie's. And then there's Mrs Martin Cohen, for making the tea as well as for never losing faith that there really were only 101 problems. [*Try to make it a bit more personal – Ed.*]

Thanks also to Lil' Sis, Big Sis, an' Middle Sis. And Ma, yes, an' Pa too. And thanks to 'Moggy' Mike Morris, 'Chocolates' Terry Diffey and, most importantly, 'Gorgeous George' MacDonald Ross, collectively the philosophers, like, of cool. And thanks to Adrian Driscoll and Tony Bruce at our esteemed publishing house, and those *crazy* refs wot looked at my book while it was just a baby. They were pretty hot, especially on that (waddyoucallit) logic stuff. Since the second edition I am pleased to 'tighten up' (as logicians might say) a bit on some of those problems involving mathematical concepts; in particular I should like to thank Moritz Becker, a very precise, but helpful, sort of German philosopher and Michael Repton.

Hey, I don't forget my arty friends from Molehill UK and the F.A.T.S. monitoring unit, who dun the pictures and found the facts. They dun it real good, too. Nor 'Ma Jon' Coupland and his computer-toting gang who created an all important virtual reality for me to finish things off in.

Hey, there's loadsa other folks too – but I don't guess I can do everyone here. But they ain't forgot.

An' I don't forget Lil' Lisa, professor of Chinese Confusion Philosophy, who presented me with a *very* interesting personal problem, which, like the best of the others, I guess I ain't solved yet.

Index

grid illusion 145, 146
Groundwork to the Metaphysics of Morals, by Kant 203
gruebleen 81

H

Hafele and Keating, light experiment. 147
hairdresser (barber) paradox 5, 118
hanging judge paradox 2, 115
Head of a Young Girl, painting by Matisse 174–5
health education 27–9
Hegel, G. W. H. 214
Hergé 142
Hobbes, Thomas 125–6
Hsun Tzu 177
Human Genome Project 172
human nature 152–3; *see also* dispositions; Job, story of; evil
Hume, David 61, 125, 148, 149, 165, 187, 198, **201-2**
Husserl, Edmund 161–2
Huxley, Aldous 172

I

idealism *see esse est percipi*
identity *see* Sorites problem; personal identity; Frege
immunisation, ethics of 25–6; *see also* three embryos problem
in vitro fertilisation 89, 172
incompleteness theorem, Gödel's 134
inference 206
infinity 34, 39, 131–2; *see also* Poincaré's problem
Inquiry, by Thomas Reid 162
introspection 61

J

James, William 177

Job, story of 175–6
Johns, 'Captain' W. E. 183
Juchen, Zheng 142

K

Kaniszsa Square 140–1
Kant, Immanuel 130, 155, 167, 202
Kaufman, Stuart 188
Kenny, Anthony 177
King of France problem 81, 161–2
knowledge 202, **203-4,** 204
as justified true belief 116
Komar, Vitaly 138

L

language and linguistics 217 –8, 222; and statements, self-referential 118
Lao Tzu 211
Laplace, Pierre Simon 130
Leibniz, Göttfried 151, 168, 201
Lévi-Strauss, Claude 217
liar paradox 122
light, nature of 103–5; speed of 102, 107, 147, 178–9, 182, 199; and two slits experiment 103–4
line point 137
Locke, John 61, 126, 153, **204**
logic **205;** Aristotle's laws of reason 194, 205; formal 111, 205–7; logical relationships 162; modern 208–9; and validity 184–5
Logical Positivists 186–7, 209
love 183
Lucretius' spear 134–5

M

Malcom, Norman 152
Martian Water problem 81, 164–5
mathematics *see* Euclid; geometry; infinity; numbers
Matisse, Henri 174–5

Index

BD
21
.C635
2007